TOP **10**
COPENHAGEN

ANTONIA CUNNINGHAM

DK
EYEWITNESS TRAVEL

Left **Amalienborg Slotsplads** Right **Houses along Nyhavn**

LONDON, NEW YORK,
MELBOURNE, MUNICH AND DELHI
www.dk.com

Printed and bound in China by Leo Paper
Products Ltd

First American edition, 2007
15 16 17 18 10 9 8 7 6 5 4 3 2 1
Published in the United States by
DK Publishing, 345 Hudson Street,
New York, NY 10014

**Copyright 2007, 2015 ©
Dorling Kindersley Limited**

**Reprinted with revisions 2009, 2011,
2013, 2015**

ISSN 1479-344X
ISBN: 978-1-46542-647-5

Within each Top 10 list in this book, no
hierarchy of quality or popularity is implied.
All 10 are, in the editor's opinion, of
roughly equal merit.

MIX
Paper from
responsible sources
FSC™ C018179
www.fsc.org

Contents

Copenhagen's Top 10

Copenhagen's Highlights   6

Harbour Sights   8

Tivoli   10

Rosenborg Slot
and Kongens Have   14

The Latin Quarter   16

Kongens Nytorv
and Nyhavn   18

Amalienborg and
Frederiksstaden   20

Statens Museum
for Kunst   22

Ny Carlsberg
Glyptotek   24

Nationalmuseet   26

Slotsholmen   28

Moments in History   32

COVER: Front – **4CORNER IMAGES**: Alberto Biscaro main. **ALAMY IMAGES**: FAN travelstock/Michael
Schindel bl. Spine – **DK IMAGES**: Dorota and Mariusz Jarymowiczowie b. Back – **DK IMAGES**: Demetrio
Carrasco tc; Rowan Greenwood tl; Dorota & Mariusz Jarymowiczowie tr.

Left **Interior of Vor Frue Kirke** Right **Designmuseum Denmark**

Museums and Galleries   34

Historic Buildings   36

Hans Christian Andersen
Sights   38

Churches   40

Performing Art and
Music Venues   42

Outdoor Activities   44

Shopping Districts   46

Restaurants   48

Cafés and Bars   50

Nightlife Venues   52

Gay and Lesbian Venues   54

Places for Children   56

Sights of Royal
Copenhagen   58

Around Town

Tivoli North to
Gothersgade   62

Nørrebro, Østerbro and
North of Gothersgade   74

Vesterbro and
Frederiksberg   82

Christianshavn and
Holmen   88

Beyond Copenhagen   96

Streetsmart

Practical Information   106

Places To Stay   112

General Index   118

Phrase Book   126

Selected Street Index   128

Left **New Year fireworks at Tivoli** Right **Café culture on Nytorv**

COPENHAGEN'S
TOP 10

Copenhagen's
Highlights
6–7

Harbour Sights
8–9

Tivoli
10–13

Rosenborg Slot and
Kongens Have
14–15

The Latin Quarter
16–17

Kongens Nytorv and
Nyhavn
18–19

Amalienborg and
Frederiksstaden
20–21

Statens Museum
for Kunst
22–23

Ny Carlsberg Glyptotek
24–25

Nationalmuseet
26–27

Slotsholmen
28–29

Top Ten of Everything
32–59

COPENHAGEN'S TOP 10

⑩ Copenhagen's Highlights

A kaleidoscope of history, culture and contemporary entertainment, Copenhagen is a vibrant capital city offering an incredible array of experiences. Walk through the cobbled streets of a medieval city, explore world-class museums, experience the finest restaurants and hippest nightlife, or simply unwind beside the gorgeous waters of a peaceful seaside town. Copenhagen has a compact centre that can easily be seen on foot and is also a great city for cycling. This charming destination has something for everyone.

Harbour Sights 1

The best way to soak up the city's plentiful and beautiful harbour sights is to take a boat trip, from Nyhavn through the Inner Harbour, along the canals of Slotsholmen and Christianshavn. It is also a fantastic way to understand Copenhagen's development over the years *(see pp8–9)*.

Tivoli 2

This pleasure garden and fun fair attracts kids and adults alike. At night, it turns especially magical with sparkling fairy lights and Chinese lanterns. The rides are brilliant for an adrenaline rush, and if you feel peckish head to one of the many restaurants *(see pp10–13)*.

Rosenborg Slot & Kongens Have 3

Set in one of Copenhagen's prettiest parks, the 17th-century Rosenborg Castle houses the royal collection, including the spectacular Crown Jewels in the basement *(see pp14–15)*.

The Latin Quarter 4

One of the oldest areas in Copenhagen, the Latin Quarter is just off the main pedestrianized street, Strøget. It is home to the university and the few medieval buildings in the city *(see pp16–17)*.

Preceding pages: **Colourful houses lining Nyhavn.**

Kongens Nytorv and Nyhavn

Kongens Nytorv (King's New Square) is a splendid Baroque square at the top of Nyhavn. Previously a seedy haunt for sailors, complete with drinking dens and brothels, Nyhavn has been transformed radically since the 1970s. It is now a popular waterside attraction with numerous restaurants and bars *(see pp18–19)*.

Amalienborg

Home to the royal family since 1794, this complex of palaces represents some of the best Rococo architecture in Denmark. The museum housed in Christian VIII's palace has some fascinating displays *(see pp20–21)*.

Statens Museum for Kunst

You will find a wonderful collection of Danish and European sculpture and paintings at the national gallery. It is housed in a 19th-century building, connected by a glass bridge to a modern wing. The museum is situated in a pleasant green park *(see pp22–3)*.

Ny Carlsberg Glyptotek

This beautifully modernized 19th-century museum is a definite must-see. It includes wonderful ancient Egyptian, Roman and Mediterranean works of art. The new wing boasts an impressive collection of French Impressionist and Post-Impressionist art *(see pp24–5)*.

Nationalmuseet

Here is a perfect example of how brilliantly the Danes design their museums. Formerly a palace, the museum now houses collections devoted to Danish history. You will also find fabulous ethnographic artifacts from around the world, as well as an excellent children's museum *(see pp26–7)*.

Slotsholmen

This is where it all began in the 12th century, when Bishop Absalon built a castle here (you can still see its remains). The present Neo-Baroque castle was built in 1907–28, but was never inhabited by the monarch. It is now shared between the royal family and the Parliament *(see pp28–9)*.

Discover more at www.dk.com

🔟 Harbour Sights

A harbour tour is a delightful way to take in the city's brilliant views and varied topography. You will be taken along the wide waters of the Inner Harbour and winding waterways of Christianshavn, then round to Slotsholmen (the island on which the original town of Havn flourished in the 12th century). Vor Frelsers Kirke, in particular, makes a spectacular sight as you look up through the rigging of sailing boats dotting the Christianshavn canal.

Den Sorte Diamant
3 The Black Diamond *(above)* a vast, eye-catching structure, holds all the books ever published in Denmark (some 6 million). It is the largest library in the Nordic countries, and a great place to find original Danish texts.

Operaen

🌀 Stromma and Netto Boats offer guided canal and harbour tours. Public harbour buses include the 901 and 902 from Den Sorte Diamant, Knippelsbro, Nyhavn, Operaen, Nyholm or Larsen Plads. Buses 991, 992 and 993 travel between Refshaleøen (Holmen) and Langelinie. Copenhagen Cards are accepted *(see p111)*.

• Map L4 • Stromma Canal Tours: 32 66 00 00; open 9:30am–6pm; adm for adults 75 Dkr, children 35 Dkr (under 6 years free); boats every 30 mins; tours in several languages (see www.stromma.dk for info) • Netto Boats: 32 54 41 02; open 10am–5pm Mar–Oct (Oct–Mar Sat–Sun only); adm for adults 40 Dkr, children 15 Dkr; boats 2–5 times an hour; tours in English, German and Danish; www.netto-baadene.dk

Top 10 Attractions
1. Operaen
2. Nyhavn
3. Den Sorte Diamant
4. Langelinie
5. Havnebadet
6. *The Little Mermaid*
7. Trekroner
8. The Canals
9. Houseboats
10. Pavilions and the Royal Yacht

Operaen
1 The incredible Opera House *(above left)* was built in just four years. Its massive, orange-maple coloured auditorium seats 1,700 people. The amazing sculptures in the foyer change colour with the weather.

Nyhavn
2 Even today, the charming old harbour of Nyhavn *(above)* is filled with boats. The old brothels and pubs have now been turned into respectable bars and restaurants serving traditional Danish dishes.

Langelinie
4 One of Copenhagen's most scenic areas, this is a wonderful place to walk along the harbour banks. Stroll past Kastellet and *The Little Mermaid*, right up to the final stretch where there is a busy cruise ship terminal *(below)*.

Inderhavnen (Inner Harbour) runs through central Copenhagen; Øresund (the Sound) separates Denmark and Sweden.

Havnebadet

Take a refreshing dip in the sparkling clean harbour waters of this popular open-air pool *(above)*, while enjoying superb views of the city. Located at Islands Brygge, there are three pools to choose from – for adults, children and a pool for divers. They are separated from each other – and from the harbour waters – by floating bridges.

Pavilions and the Royal Yacht

On the quayside, just beyond *The Little Mermaid*, are two green-domed pavilions *(below)*. It is here that the Danish royal family gathers before boarding their stunning 79-m (259-ft) royal yacht, called the *Dannebrog*, which shares its name with the Danish flag (said to have fallen from the sky in the year 1219). Launched in 1931, the yacht is crewed by nine officers, seven sergeants and 36 seamen: an improvement on the earlier royal ship, a paddle steamer dating back to the year 1879.

The Canals

The canals that you glide along on the tour *(above)* were built in a Dutch style in 1618 at the command of Christian IV. It is because of this that Christianshavn is some-times also referred to as "Little Amsterdam".

The Little Mermaid

Den Lille Havfrue (above) is a surprisingly small landmark, ordered by brewery magnate Carl Jacobsen in 1909. It was created in 1913 by Edvard Eriksen, whose wife, Eline, was the model.

Trekroner

This 18th-century fort has been used only once: on 1 April 1801, during the Battle of Copenhagen, when firing against the British fleet. Second in command of the fleet was Admiral Lord Nelson.

Houseboats

The houseboats *(above)* along the canals have an eclectic mix of styles, ranging from conventional boat-like structures to some with barge-like designs, and other modern, funky homes built on floating platforms, complete with outdoor spaces.

Mutant Mermaid

Close to *The Little Mermaid*, almost inviting controversy, sits a group of sculptures called *Paradise Genetically Altered*. Designed by Bjørn Nørgaard, it comprises a triumphal arch, with a 9-m (29-ft), genetically altered Madonna atop it, surrounded by Adam, Eve, Christ, Mary Magdalene, a critical representation of capitalism and a pregnant man. On its own small island is the *Genetically Modified Little Mermaid*. It is a surreal take on *The Little Mermaid* perched a short distance away.

For hotels with water views, **see p117;** *and for days out by the Sound,* **see pp96–103.**

🔟 Tivoli

Famous for its fairy-tale ambience, exotic buildings, gorgeous landscaped gardens and up-market entertainment and restaurants, the Tivoli Gardens are more than an amusement park. The atmosphere is magical enough to merit a visit even if you are not interested in the excellent rides on offer. Founded in 1843, Tivoli has long been a favourite with royalty. It also proved to be a great source of inspiration for Walt Disney when he visited in the 1950s.

Thrill Rides
Day or night, Tivoli rings with the shrieks of people whizzing along on thrill rides such as *Aquila, The Demon (above), Vertigo* and *The Starflyer,* which reaches a height of 80m (262 ft).

Tivoli Gardens

🍃 Go on the thrill rides during the day, when it's more family-oriented, as queues can build up in the evenings.

🍽 Enjoy a meal at one of the restaurants here *(see pp12–13).*

- Map H5
- Vesterbrogade 3
- 33 15 10 01
- Open mid-Apr–Sep 11am–10pm (11pm in Jul) Mon–Thu & Sun, 11am–12:30am Fri, 11am–midnight Sat
- Adm for adults and children 8 years and over 99 Dkr; free for under-8s
- Dis access
- www.tivoli.dk

Top 10 Features

1. Thrill Rides
2. Gentle Rides
3. Traditional Rides
4. Dragon Boats
5. Tivoli at Night
6. Pantomime Theatre
7. Tivoli Concert Hall and Open-Air Stage
8. Tivoli Akvarium
9. Tivoli Boys' Guard
10. Nimb Hotel

Gentle Rides
For children and the faint-hearted, there are plenty of fun, gentle rides. *The Ferris wheel* is an observation wheel that offers great views over Tivoli. You could also enjoy an old-fashioned trolley-bus ride, a traditional carousel *(above)* with exotic animals and music, a waltzer in the shape of a pirate ship and several charming kids' rides, such as flying dragons and miniature classic cars.

Traditional Rides
Tivoli's current *Ferris wheel (below)* dates from 1943. *The Roller Coaster* (1914), one of the oldest of its kind, reaches speeds of 36 mph (58 km/h).

4 Dragon Boats

These boats *(below)* are very popular rides at Tivoli. Kids love floating on the lake during the day. In the evenings, the setting turns romantic.

5 Tivoli at Night

Sparkling resplendently with thousands of fairy lights and Chinese lanterns, Tivoli is magical at night. You can catch the dazzling Tivoli Illuminations show *(right)* over the lake, an exuberant, late-night presentation involving fireworks, laser lights, music and waterjets.

6 Pantomime Theatre

Built in 1874, this theatre has an exotic Chinese design and a spectacular stage curtain styled like a peacock's tail *(left)*. It is known for its enjoyable mime shows, performed in the commedia dell'arte tradition.

7 Tivoli Concert Hall and Open-Air Stage

The hall hosts varied performances, from classical to pop. There is music daily in the Harmony Pavilion, and free open-air rock concerts on Friday nights.

8 Tivoli Akvarium

Don't miss the amazing aquarium *(above)* in the foyer of the Concert Hall. Based on a tropical coral reef, this extensive salt-water aquarium is home to more than 1,600 fish (over 500 varieties). Among the popular attractions are the rays and huge moray eels.

Christmas at Tivoli

Tivoli opens for six weeks between mid-November and the end of December for a winter wonderland: a no-holds-barred, elf-driven, Father Christmas-strewn, illuminated Christmas extravaganza that you won't forget in a hurry! A similar Halloween celebration takes place in mid-October.

9 Tivoli Boys' Guard

A tradition since 1844, the Boys' Guard parades through Tivoli, complete with instruments, coach and horses – a delightful picture, befitting the home city of that master of fairy tales, H C Andersen.

10 Nimb Hotel

This splendid hotel, housed in the Nimb building *(centre)*, offers a variety of culinary experiences, such as a *vinoteque,* the Andersen Bakery, a Bar'n'Grill with primed steaks and a brasserie restaurant.

For more places that children will enjoy, see pp56–7.

Left **Nimb Brasserie** Centre **Grill Royal** Right **Mazzoli's Caffè & Trattoria**

Tivoli Restaurants

Grill Royal
The Tivoli branch of the local Madklubben group of restaurants offers steaks, burgers and *moules-frites* in a barbecue-heavy menu. Children's menu available and open-air rock concerts on Fridays. ◈ *33 75 07 55 • Open noon–midnight (kitchen closes 10pm) during Tivoli season • ⓚⓚ*

Nimb Brasserie
European bistro classics are given a modern face-lift in this informal, upscale restaurant in relaxed surroundings. Diners can come here for breakfast, lunch and dinner. ◈ *Bernstorffsgade 5 • 88 70 00 10 • Open 7am–10pm daily • www.nimb.dk • ⓚⓚⓚⓚ*

Mazzoli's Caffè & Trattoria
Italian cuisine is served in this pretty, circular building that was originally built as a dance hall in 1883. ◈ *33 75 07 51 • www.mazzolis.dk • ⓚⓚ*

Nimb Terrasse
Highly regarded Nimb Terrasse offers tasteful French-Scandinavian dishes in a light, airy bistro setting. There is a special seafood barbecue during summer months.
◈ *33 75 07 50 • Open noon–4pm & 5:30pm–midnight (kitchen closes 10pm) during Tivoli season • ⓚⓚⓚⓚ*

Woodhouse
A family-friendly burger and soft-ice joint on the first floor of the old wooden "Valhalla" building. The downstairs lounge caters more for the party crowd. ◈ *Vesterbrogade 3 • 33 75 07 41 • ⓚ*

Det Japanske Tårn
This exotic Tivoli icon on the lake makes a spectacular picture, especially when it is lit up at night. The former Chinese Tower offers sushi, teriyaki and other Japanese and Asian cuisine. ◈ *33 33 78 00 • www.detjapansketaarn.dk • ⓚⓚⓚ*

Det Japanske Tårn

Færgekroen Bryghus
Færgekroen, one of Tivoli's oldest restaurants, has been made over into a modern space, with its own brewery. The rustic charm has been preserved, while the traditional Danish food complements the fine ales. ◈ *33 75 06 80 • www.faergekroen.com • ⓚⓚⓚ*

Wagamama
One of Copenhagen's cheapest restaurants, this trendy chain offering excellent Japanese fare is situated in the complex at the Tivoli Concert Hall. It can get very busy, so you may find yourself sharing a table with strangers. ◈ *33 75 06 58 • www.wagamama.dk • ⓚ*

For a key to the price categories, see pp67.

Hereford Beefstouw

The flagship restaurant in a chain of up-market steakhouses, the Hereford Beefstouw is a mecca for people who love steak and beer. The steaks are cooked just right and are of first-class quality with prices to match. Its micro-brewery, the Apollo, stands right in the centre of the restaurant.

Stegt Flæsk

🔊 33 12 74 41 • Open 11:30am–3pm & 5–10:30pm daily • www.a-h-b.dk/eng • ⓚⓚⓚⓚ

Italia – La Vecchia Signora

This cheerful Italian restaurant is well known for its stone-baked pizzas, all produced in traditional ovens specially imported from Sardinia, Italy. The rest of the menu includes home-made pasta topped with a variety of sauces, carpaccio, mussels in parsley and garlic, fresh fish of the day, meat dishes and authentic Italian desserts. 🔊 33 75 09 75 • Children's menu available • ⓚⓚ

Top 10 Historic Tivoli Events

1. 1843: Tivoli opens with a horse-drawn carousel and a roller coaster.
2. 1944: The Nazis blow up part of Tivoli in order to crush Danish morale.
3. 1950: Walt Disney visits Tivoli and is inspired to create his own park.
4. 1956: The Concert Hall opens, then the largest in Northern Europe.
5. 1978: The New York City Ballet and its founder, George Balanchine, visit.
6. 1994: Tivoli's Christmas season is launched.
7. 2000: Hosts the 60th birthday celebrations for the Queen.
8. 2006: Launch of The Starflyer, one of the world's tallest carousels.
9. 2008: The Nimb empire re-opens in Tivoli's Moorish bazaar.
10. 2010: Tivoli becomes the first amusement park in the world to be run on renewable wind energy.

The Founding of Tivoli

The creation of the Tivoli Gardens can be credited to Georg Carstensen, a man who persuaded the Danish king, Christian VIII, to grant him a five-year charter by saying, "When the people are amusing themselves, they do not think about politics." Mindful of this fact, Christian VIII granted him 6 ha (15 acres) of land outside the city walls. Carstensen, who had been brought up in the Middle East, provided Oriental-style buildings, cafés, restaurants and, in the early days, a horse-drawn carousel and a roller coaster. Brilliant fireworks further enlivened this magnificent amusement area. It was named Tivoli after the Jardins de Tivoli in Paris, which were themselves named after a place called Tivoli just outside Rome. The gardens inspired Walt Disney greatly when he visited; in fact, he was so impressed by them he exclaimed to his wife, "Now this is what an amusement place should be!"

Tivoli at night

For more restaurants in the Tivoli area, **see pp67 and 71.**

🔟 Rosenborg Slot and Kongens Have

Complete with fairy-tale turrets and bronze lions guarding the entrance, Rosenborg Castle was originally built as a summer house in 1606–34 by Christian IV. At that time, it stood surrounded by sprawling gardens (now the Kongens Have park) out in the tranquil countryside. This was Christian IV's favourite castle and like other monarchs after him, he spent much of his time here. When he was on his deathbed at Frederiksborg Castle in 1648, he insisted on being brought to Rosenborg Castle, and eventually died here.

Rosenborg Slot

✪ Avoid lurking near the guards at the entrance to the Crown Jewels – you might be considered a security risk.

🍴 There is a restaurant and a small café in Kongens Have, but you will enjoy yourself a lot more if you have a picnic on the lawn or on one of the many benches in the garden.

- Map J2
- Øster Voldgade 4A
- 33 15 32 86
- Open Nov–Apr: 10am–2pm Tue–Sun; May, Sep & Oct: 10am–4pm daily; Jun–Aug: 10am–5pm daily
- Adm for adults 90 Dkr, students 60 Dkr, senior citizens 55 Dkr, free for under-18s; Kongens Have gardens free; Copenhagen Card accepted (see p111)
- Guided tours (1–1½ hr long) in English, German and French (advance booking required)
- www.dkks.dk
- www.rosenborgslot.dk

Top 10 Features

1. Rosenborg Slot
2. Crown Jewels
3. Winter Room
4. Christian IV's Bedroom
5. Dark Room
6. Marble Hall
7. Frederik IV's Chamber Room
8. Glass Cabinet
9. Knight's Hall
10. Kongens Have

Rosenborg Slot
The castle's 24 rooms occupy three floors. Most of them retain the original Renaissance decor from Christian IV's residence; the rest were redecorated by later kings. The last king to live here permanently was Frederik IV. In 1838, the castle became the first royal residence to open to the public.

Crown Jewels
The castle has been used as the treasury of the realm since 1658. In the castle's basement, behind heavily guarded security doors, are Denmark's Crown Jewels (*above*), which include Christian IV's diamond-encrusted crown (*see p59*).

Winter Room
This panelled room is said to have been one of Christian IV's most important private chambers. Look out for the speaking tubes that connect with the wine cellar and room above.

Christian IV's Bedroom
Another private apartment, Christian IV's bloodied clothing, from the naval battle of Kolberger Heide (1644) where he lost an eye, are found here. The king wanted these clothes preserved as national mementos.

Dark Room

5 This room is filled with fascinating objects, such as the startling wax portraits of Frederik III, and the 17th-century "trick" chair that grasped unsuspecting occupants with tentacles and soaked them in water. A trumpet played when they finally stood up.

Marble Hall

6 Originally the bedroom of Kirsten Munk, Christian IV's morganatic wife, Frederik III turned it into a Baroque show of splendour *(below)* to celebrate the introduction of Absolute Monarchy.

Frederik IV's Chamber Room

7 In the 1700s, this room was used by Frederik IV's sister, Sophie Hedvig, as an antechamber and the tapestries that hang here date back to this period. Look for the intricate equestrian statue of Frederik, made from silver. The coffered ceiling *(below)* is the original from the time of Christian IV.

Glass Cabinet

8 This room was designed as a glass cabinet in 1713–14 by Frederik IV. The cabinet was built to house the extensive collection of glassware presented to Frederik in 1709 by the city of Venice. Porcelain cabinets were common in 17th-century Europe but this is the only known glass one and was inspired by the porcelain cabinet at Berlin's Charlottenburg Palace.

Knight's Hall

9 Known as the Long Hall before 1750, this room was completed in 1624 as a celebration hall. Only two Dutch fireplaces remain from the original decorations. Note the beautiful white stucco ceiling, Frederik III's astonishing "unicorn"-horn throne (1660s), guarded by silver lions, and the solid-silver, Baroque furniture.

Kongens Have

10 Visited by over 2 million people every year, these are Denmark's oldest royal gardens and date back to the 17th century. There is a rose garden, which contains many statues, including a large one of Queen Caroline Amalie that was created by Vilhelm Bissen. Elsewhere in the grounds, at the end of one of the paths, is a statue of Hans Christian Andersen. The park also has the Renaissance garden Krumspringet and a fanciful playground. Various art events and a puppet theatre for children are held here during summer.

Rosenborg's Kings

Christian IV, 1588–1648: Built many of Copenhagen's Renaissance buildings.
Frederik III, 1648–1670: Introduced Absolute Monarchy to curb the aristocracy's power.
Christian V, 1670–1699: Introduced fairer taxation.
Frederik IV, 1699–1730: Built Frederiksborg Castle, among other well-known buildings.
Christian VI, 1730–1746: Known as the religious king.
Frederik V, 1746–1766: Responsible for the building of the Frederiksstaden district.

For more royal sights, **see pp58–9.**

⏰10 The Latin Quarter

The Latin Quarter is home to Copenhagen's university, where Latin used to be the spoken language. One of the oldest areas in the city, it is full of 17th-century buildings that were built by the architect king, Christian IV. Although there have been dwellings here since medieval times, most of them were destroyed in the disastrous fire that spread across Copenhagen in 1728 (see p33). Today, the Latin Quarter is a lively and bustling student area brimming with shops and cafés.

Universitetet

🕐 This area is known for its hip, alternative shops.

🔵 Studenterhuset, opposite Regensen, is a cheap option.

• Map H4
• Helligåndskirken: Niels Hemmingsens Gade 5; 33 15 41 44; open noon–4pm Mon–Fri, (7pm–midnight Fri)
• Synagogen: Krystalgade 12; 33 12 88 68
• Rundetårn, Trinitatis Kirke: Købmagergade 52A; 33 73 03 73; Tower: open Jun–Aug: 10am–8pm daily; Sep–May: 10am–6pm daily; www.rundetaarn.dk; adm free with Copenhagen Card Church: open 9:30am–4:30pm Mon–Sat; www.trinitatiskirke.dk
• Universitetet: Nørregade 10; 35 32 26 26; open 9am–5pm Mon–Fri; www.ku.dk/english/
• Vor Frue Kirke: Nørregade 8; open 8am–5pm Mon–Sat
• Sankt Petri Kirke: Skt Peders St 2; 33 13 38 33; open Apr–Sep: 11am–3pm Tue–Sat; adm to sepulchral chapel

Top 10 Features

1. Helligåndskirken
2. Synagogen
3. Rundetårn
4. Universitetet
5. Trinitatis Kirke
6. Vor Frue Kirke
7. Sankt Petri Kirke
8. Regensen
9. Højbro Plads
10. Gråbrødretorv

Helligåndskirken
The Church of the Holy Ghost *(below)* was first built in 1295 as a hospital for the weak and elderly, and expanded to include a monastery in 1474. The west-wing Helligåndshuset is the city's only preserved medieval building.

Rundetårn

The Round Tower was built in 1642 by Christian IV as an observatory, its official role until 1861. It is 34.8 m (114 ft) high, with an internal ramp that spirals almost to the top *(below)*. Open to the public, it holds art exhibitions and concerts in the library hall, where there is a pleasant café.

Synagogen
Copenhagen's oldest synagogue (1833) is one of the few in Europe to have survived Nazi occupation. The main synagogue for the city's Jewish community, it is not open to visitors except with prior booking.

➡ *Tsar Peter of Russia supposedly rode his horse to the top of the Rundetårn in 1716, his wife following in a coach and six.*

Universitetet
Founded in 1479 by Christian I, the University of Copenhagen was Denmark's first university. The Neo-Classical building *(left)* that stands here today is from the 19th century. In the courtyard, there are the remains of an old Bishop's Palace (1420). Disorderly students used to be put in its cellar as punishment. Most of the university is now on the island of Amager.

Trinitatis Kirke
This magnificent church *(centre)* was built in 1637–56 for the staff and students of the university. If it happens to be closed when you visit, you could enter Rundetårn and look down the church nave through the glass panel at the start of the ramp.

Vor Frue Kirke
In the 12th century, Bishop Absalon founded a Gothic church on this site. After burning down twice, the present Neo-Classical cathedral *(above)* was completed in 1829, but the tower is from medieval times. One of the bells is Denmark's oldest (1490) and another (weighing 4 tonnes) is the biggest.

Sankt Petri Kirke
Older than Vor Frue Kirke, Copenhagen's German church also suffered from city fires and the British bombardment (1807). Its vaulted sepulchral chapel has monuments and tombs dating back to 1681.

Regensen
Opposite the Rundetårn, this student residence was built in the 17th century. It burned down in the great fire of 1728, but was rebuilt not long after. Even today, the students retain several old traditions, including "storming" Rundetårn every May.

Højbro Plads
The equestrian statue *(left)* on this popular square depicts Bishop Absalon, founder of Copenhagen, pointing towards the site of his original castle on Slotsholmen.

Gråbrødretorv
Named after the Grey Brothers who built Copenhagen's first monastery here, this 13th-century square is now a popular place to eat in the open air.

The Bells and Carillon of Helligåndskirken

In 1647, 50 years after the clock tower was built, architect king Christian IV gifted the church a set of bells and a grand carillon. The carillon consisted of 19 bells and chimed a verse from a hymn every 30 minutes. It was also used at funerals; the importance of the deceased depended on the duration for which it played. This was at times taken too far; as playwright Ludwig Holberg (1684–1754) said when the carillon played for 4 straight hours: "A soul need not be so long on its way to heaven as the mail horse is to Roskilde". They were destroyed in the fire of 1728.

For more information on shops in the area and along nearby Strøget, see pp68–9.

🔟 Kongens Nytorv and Nyhavn

Kongens Nytorv (King's New Square) and Nyhavn (New Harbour) are two of the most picturesque areas in Copenhagen. It's hard to imagine the square was once outside the city gates and the site of the town gallows in medieval times. The Nyhavn canal was planned by Frederik III to connect the Inner Harbour with the square, enabling merchants to unload their goods more easily. The canal area is full of colourful houses and the bars and cafés come alive with visitors in summer.

Equestrian statue

⚫ The bars and restaurants on the south side of Nyhavn are usually not as busy as those on the north.

🔵 Find a quick bite away from the crowds in Nyhavn Pizzeria at 8 Lille Strandstræde.
• Map K4–L4

• *Charlottenborg Slot: Nyhavn 2; 33 13 40 22; open 11am–5pm Tue–Sun (until 8pm Wed); adm 60 Dkr, seniors and students 40 Dkr; free with Copenhagen Card; www.kunsthal charlottenborg.dk*
• *Amber Museum: Kongens Nytorv 2; 33 11 67 00; open May–Sep: 10am–6:30pm daily; Oct–Apr: 10am–5:30pm daily; adm; www.houseof amber.com* • *Magasin du Nord: Kongens Nytorv 13; open 10am–8pm daily; www.magasin.dk*
• *Det Kongelige Teater: Kongens Nytorv; 33 69 69 33; guided tours available, book at the box office or in advance; www.kglteater.dk*

Top 10 Features

1. Nyhavn
2. Nyhavn Nos 18, 20 and 67
3. Equestrian Statue
4. Hotel d'Angleterre
5. Charlottenborg Slot
6. Det Kongelige Teater
7. Magasin du Nord
8. Vingårdsstræde 6
9. Store Strandestræde and Lille Strandstræde
10. Amber Museum

1 Nyhavn
Running down to the Inner Harbour, this canal *(right)* is flanked by 18th-century houses that belonged to merchants. A large anchor, in honour of sailors who lost their lives in Word War II, marks the starting point of Nyhavn.

2 Nyhavn Nos 18, 20 and 67
These brightly painted merchants' houses *(below)* were built at the same time as the harbour. Fairy-tale writer H C Andersen lived in them. He wrote his first tale, *The Tinder Box* (1835), at No 20.

3 Equestrian Statue
The bronze statue in the middle of Kongens Nytorv commemorates Christian V (1646–99), who rebuilt the square in 1670 in Baroque style. Sculpted by the Frenchman Lamoureux, it shows the king dressed as a Roman emperor.

4 Hotel d'Angleterre
This is Copenhagen's oldest hotel (1755), and one of the oldest in the world. It has played host to royalty and countless celebrities, including Karen Blixen, Winston Churchill, Grace Kelly and Madonna.

Charlottenborg Slot

An early example of the Danish Baroque style, this palace *(right)* was built by Frederik III's illegitimate son Ulrik in 1672–83. Today it houses the Royal Danish Academy of Fine Arts and Kunsthal Charlottenborg, a contemporary art museum. Walk along the north side of Nyhavn for a better view of the palace walls and to enter the courtyard.

Det Kongelige Teater
This Baroque-style theatre is the third one to stand on this site since 1749. It is home to the Royal Danish Ballet company.

Vingårdsstræde 6
Hans Christian Andersen lived in the attic room of No 6 Vingårdsstræde for a year at the age of 22. The building is one of the oldest in Copenhagen. Its 13th-century wine cellars (there used to be a vineyard here, hence *Vingårdsstræde*) now house a Michelin-starred restaurant, Kong Hans Kælder *(left)*.

Store Strandstræde and Lille Strandstræde
Once full of seedy pubs and brothels, "Big Beach Street" and "Little Beach Street" are now home to sophisticated art galleries and stylish designer-wear shops. For a taste of its past, there are a few tattoo parlours dotted around the area.

Amber Museum

Set in a house dating back to 1606, this museum *(right)* displays an exquisite collection dedicated to Denmark's national gem, amber (also called Nordic Gold). You will find amber antiques, prehistoric pieces and an 8.8-kg (19-lb) amber stone. Amber jewellery is also sold at a shop on the premises.

Magasin du Nord
Originally the famous Hotel du Nord, this is Copenhagen's oldest department store *(left)* and is considered to be the city's answer to London's Selfridges or New York's Bloomingdale's. Standing on the north side of Kongens Nytorv, the store will strike you as an impressive sight when you pass by. A range of restaurants are scattered throughout the building. Make sure you pay a visit to the Food Hall that is housed in the basement of the department store. The menu features a wide variety of delicious preparations that are worth sampling.

"The Imperial Ethiopian Palace" in Copenhagen

In the 1950s, Ethopia's Emperor Haile Selassie (also known as the King of Kings or the Conquering Lion of the Tribe of Judah), his wife and their entire family and entourage, visited Denmark's king and queen. In Copenhagen for only a few days, they stayed at the plush and luxurious Hotel d'Angleterre. A grand banquet was held in honour of Denmark's royal visitors in the Louis XVI Hall. During the time of their stay in the hotel, all telephone calls were answered with, "The Imperial Ethiopian Palace".

🕙 Amalienborg and Frederiksstaden

Built in the 1750s, this stately complex was designed by the royal architect, Nicolai Eigtved. Four Rococo palaces, originally home to four noble families, are set around an octagonal square in Frederiksstaden, an artistocratic area built by Frederik V. Christian VII bought the palaces after the Christiansborg Palace burned down in 1794. The royal family has lived here ever since. It was named after a palace built on this site by Queen Sophie Amalie in the 17th century, which burned down in 1689 during a theatrical performance.

Amaliehaven

🚳 The guards will not respond well to people sitting on palace steps.

🍴 Head down Amaliegade to the bars and cafés along Nyhavn.

• Map L3 • Amalienborg Museum: 33 12 21 86; open May–Oct: 10am–4pm daily; Nov–Apr: 11am–4pm Tue–Sun; adm for adults 70 Dkr (90 Dkr on Saturdays), students 50 Dkr (60 Dkr on Saturdays), free with Copenhagen Card; www.dkks.dk/ amalienborg-palace
• Marmorkirken: Frederiksgade 4; 33 15 01 44; open 10am–7pm Mon–Thu, noon–5pm Fri–Sun; Tower mid-Jun–Aug: 1–3pm daily; Sep–mid-Jun: 1–3pm Sat–Sun; adm; www.marmor kirken.dk
• Christian VII's, Frederik VIII's and Christian IX's palaces are closed to the public

Top 10 Features

1. Christian VII's Palace
2. Christian VIII's Palace
3. Frederik VIII's Palace
4. Christian IX's Palace
5. Equestrian Statue of Frederik V
6. Marmorkirken
7. Amaliehaven
8. Palace Guards
9. The Golden Axis
10. Colonade

1 Christian VII's Palace

This palace was one of the first to be completed by the time of Eigtved's death in 1754. Also known as Moltke Palace, named after its original owner, Count Adam Gottlob Moltke, it is the most expensive palace in the complex and also has one of Denmark's best Rococo interiors. The queen often uses it to welcome foreign guests.

2 Christian VIII's Palace

This is where Crown Prince Frederik lived until his marriage to Australian Mary Donaldson in 2004. Part of the palace is open all year round as the Amalienborg Museum, dedicated to the Glücksberg Dynasty. Visit Queen Louise's chintzy drawing room and the studies of several kings.

Marmorkirken

3 Frederik VIII's Palace

Previously known as Brockdorff's Palace, this palace *(left)*, with a clock on its façade, was renamed after Frederik VIII moved into it in 1869. More recently, it was home to Queen Dowager Ingrid (Queen Margrethe's mother) till her death in 2000. Since 2010 it has been the residence of Crown Prince Frederik and Crown Princess Mary.

Discover more at www.dk.com

Christian IX's Palace

The first royal family to live here was Crown Prince Frederik VI and his wife (1794). Since 1967, it has been home to Queen Margrethe and Prince Consort Henrik.

Equestrian Statue of Frederik V

Designed and cast (1753–71) by French sculptor Jacques Saly, this statue of Frederik V is said to have cost four times as much as Amalienborg. Saly, who stayed here for 18 years, was known for the extravagant parties he hosted. His expenses were paid by the Danish Asiatic Company, who gifted this statue to the king.

Marmorkirken

Properly called Frederikskirken, the Marble Church *(centre)* got its popular name on account of plans to build it using Norwegian marble. Its dome, one of the largest in Europe and modelled after St Peter's in Rome, has a diameter of 31 m (102 ft).

Amaliehaven

The Amalie Garden was created in 1983 on the banks of the Harbour, financed by the shipping giant A P Møller and the Christine McKinney Møller Foundation. It has a splendid fountain that lies on Copenhagen's "Golden Axis" *(see below)*, between the Opera House and the statue of Frederik V.

Palace Guards

When the queen is in residence, the Danish Royal Life Guards *(right)* stand outside the palace, guarding their monarch in 2-hour shifts. At noon they are replaced by the guards from Rosenborg Castle *(see pp14–15)*, who march through the streets of Copenhagen every day at noon to switch places with the guards at Amalienborg Palace.

The Russian Connection

A stone's throw from Marmorkirken *(see p78)*, the golden onion domes of Alexander Nevsky Kirke, the Russian Orthodox Cathedral, are easily identifiable. Consecrated in 1883, it was a gift from the future Tsar Alexander III to mark his marriage to the Danish Princess Marie Dagmar in St Petersburg in 1866. It was in this church that her funeral was held when she passed away in 1928.

The Golden Axis

Marmorkirken and Frederiksstaden lie on a short axis called the Golden Axis. This axis was considered so important that when the Opera House was built along this line, it caused much controversy. The building is now considered the axis' modern extension.

Colonnade

This Classical-style colonnade *(right)* was built by Christian VII's royal architect, Caspar Frederik Harsdorff, in 1794–5. Supported by eight ionic columns, it runs unobtrusively from one palace to another.

Christian IX was called the "Father-in-law of Europe"; his children married into royal families from Sweden, Britain and Germany.

🔟 Statens Museum for Kunst

Denmark's national gallery is housed in two buildings – one dating back to the 19th century and the other, a stylish, modern extension, linked by a bridge over a sculpture gallery known as Sculpture Street. The museum's collections span international and national paintings, sculptures, installations, prints and drawings from the 14th century to the present. The national collection specializes in paintings from the Golden Age and by later 19th-century artists such as the Skagen school, the rebels of their time.

The modern extension

🍂 The children's museum provides activities every Saturday and Sunday through the summer holidays.

The department of prints and drawings has a fascinating collection dating back to the 15th century. Highlights include works by Rembrandt, Manet and Picasso.

🍴 The bright, stylish museum café looks out onto Ostre Anlæg Lake. In good weather, the park is ideal for a picnic.

• Map J2
• Sølvgade 48–50
• 33 74 84 94
• Open 10am–5pm Tue–Sun, 10am–8pm Wed, closed Mon
• Guided tours for families are also available
• Free except for special exhibitions; Copenhagen Card accepted (see p111)
• www.smk.dk

Top 10 Features

1. Sculpture Street
2. Christ as the Suffering Redeemer
3. The X-Room
4. Artemis
5. The Meeting of Joachim and Anne outside the Golden Gate of Jerusalem
6. Please, Keep Quiet!
7. Portrait of Madame Matisse
8. Alice
9. The Wheel of Life
10. Romantic Paintings

The X-Room

An experimental space with changing installations by young international artists. The black box interior is transformed into fantastic, multimedia worlds.

Sculpture Street

An impressive, varied collection of sculptures by international contemporary artists runs the entire length of the building, linking the old and new wings. The displays look resplendent beneath the sunlight streaming in through the glass roof.

Christ as the Suffering Redeemer

This striking painting (1495–1500) by prominent Renaissance artist Andrea Mantegna shows the Resurrection of Christ on the third day after his crucifixion. Mantegna is known for his profound interest in ancient Roman civilization; in this painting *(left)*, it comes through in the porphyry sarcophagus.

4 Artemis
Created in 1893-4, Vilhelm Hammershøi's painting *(right)*, shows the goddess Artemis crowned with a crescent moon. The painting's Arcadian nudity, lack of depth, muted palate and enigmatic coolness are typical of the artist's work.

5 The Meeting of Joachim and Anne outside the Golden Gate of Jerusalem
Filippino Lippi (1457–1504) was a true Renaissance artist. This is evident in the architectural detail of the Corinthian columns. Much of the other background follows a more medieval tradition and is based on his home town of Florence.

6 Please, Keep Quiet!
Visitors enter this installation by Elmgreen and Dragset (2003) through swing doors which open to an eerily lifelike scene of a four-bed hospital ward. This represents not only the sterile atmosphere of a hospital but also the neutrality of an exhibition space.

Key

▦	Ground floor
▦	First floor
▦	Second floor

7 Portrait of Madame Matisse
Also known as *The Green Stripe*, this painting by Henri Matisse of his wife was to have far-reaching repercussions in the art world. It was one of several radical paintings in the 1905 *Salon d'Automne* and helped give rise to the Fauvist movement, known for its bright colours and spontaneous style.

8 Alice
One of over 300 portraits by Amedeo Modigliani painted between 1915 and 1920, this beautiful painting reflects the artist's interest in African sculpture. He has made use of simple shapes and stylized features to create an idealized portrait.

9 The Wheel of Life
Belonging to the *Suite of Seasons* series, this painting (1953) by Asger Jorn *(see p35)* represents the month of January. Alluding to the medieval concept of "the wheel of life", Jorn, who was suffering from tuberculosis, was inspired to paint this in the hope of better health.

10 Romantic Paintings
Per Kirkeby is one of Denmark's most important living artists. This early collage from 1965 uses clippings from popular magazines and comics both as a homage to Pop Art and as a commentary on the state of romance in the late 20th century.

Museum Guide

Enter the museum from the corner of Sølvgade and Øster Voldgade. The lobby is flanked by temporary exhibitions and a bookshop. The ground floor is taken up by the Sculpture Street, with Danish and international art after 1900 in the extension of the first floor. The old main building houses European Art 1300–1800, Danish and Nordic Art 1750–1900 and French Art 1900–1930.

⁸⁴⁰ Ny Carlsberg Glyptotek

This marvellous glyptotek (which means "a collection of statues") is set inside two turn-of-the-20th-century buildings linked by a charming Winter Garden and a modern wing designed by architect Henning Larsen. It contains the world-class collections of brewer Carl Jacobsen (see p84) and his son Helge, as well as more recent additions. Exhibits range from ancient Egyptian, Greek and Roman sculpture, to early 19th- and 20th-century Danish and French art. The roof terrace affords great views of the city and Tivoli.

Museum façade

⭐ English guided tours are held in summer at 12:45pm every Tuesday to Saturday and at noon on Sunday. Tours in Danish are held at 2pm on Sunday. Free tickets are available at the ticket counter; no advance booking.

🍴 The Winter Garden has a pleasant café serving cakes and pastries. Otherwise, packed lunches can be enjoyed in the museum's basement lunch area, next to the cloakroom.

• Map H6
• Dantes Plads 7
• 33 41 81 41
• Open 11am–5pm Tue–Sun
• Adm for adults 75 Dkr, free on Sun, under 18 years free; Copenhagen Card accepted (see p111)
• www.glyptoteket.com

Top 10 Features

1. The Ancient Mediterranean Collection
2. The Greek Collection
3. The Roman Collection
4. The Egyptian Collection
5. Danish Golden Age Paintings
6. The French Impressionists
7. The Post-Impressionists
8. 19th-century French Sculpture
9. 19th-century Danish Sculpture
10. The Winter Garden

Key

▨ Ground floor
▨ First floor
▨ Second floor

The Ancient Mediterranean Collection

Located in the new wing of the museum, this collection has fascinating artifacts, particularly from the Middle East and Etruria. The most impressive pieces are the Etruscan sarcophagi dating back to the period between 200 and 150 BC.

The Greek Collection

This collection has works of art from the 6th to 1st centuries BC. A highlight is one of the earliest Attic healing-god reliefs (around 420 BC), which depicts a daughter of Hygeia, god of healing, promising health to Athenians during a plague. There is also a marble statue of Demosthenes *(left).*

The Roman Collection

There are some excellent busts of Rome's public figures in this collection, including those of luminaries such as General Pompey, Emperor Augustus, the evil and depraved Caligula and Emperor Hadrian, considered to be one of the best rulers of the empire.

4 The Egyptian Collection
Part of this collection is displayed in underground chambers into which you descend, as if into a mummy's tomb. There are also some huge sculptures *(left)*, like that of the god Ptah with King Ramesses II (1290–1224 BC). The oldest piece is a small 5,000-year-old hippo.

5 Danish Golden Age Paintings
Here you will find great works of art from Denmark's Golden Age (1800–50), a period when art and culture blossomed despite political and economic strife. The greatest artists of the period, Eckersberg, Købke and Lundbye, are especially well represented.

6 The French Impressionists
This collection includes paintings by Manet, Renoir, Sisley, Monet and Pissarro, among a host of other artists. The *Absinthe Drinker* by Manet is a particular highlight, as is the remarkable Degas bronze ballerina *(right)*.

7 The Post-Impressionists
This splendid gallery holds early works by artists like Van Gogh *(right)* and Cézanne, as well as the world's largest collection of Gauguin paintings.

8 19th-century French Sculpture
This stunning collection features the biggest names in French sculpture, including Rodin *(left)*, Barye, Maillol, Carpeaux, Dubois and Falguière.

9 19th-century Danish Sculpture
This collection includes works by Neo-Classical sculptors like Villhelm Bissen and Jens Jerichau. Bissen's *Danaid* (1880) epitomizes Neo-Classical style.

10 The Winter Garden
This glass-domed garden is a great place to relax amid statues, including *The Water Mother* (1921), by Danish sculptor Kai Nielsen.

Museum Guide
Enter the museum from H C Andersens Boulevard. Buy tickets downstairs. On the far left of the central Winter Garden is the entrance to the Larsen building and the French Impressionist collection. Walk through the Winter Garden and up a few steps to the grand Central Hall, with its collection of Greek, Roman and Egyptian antiquities. The 19th-century Danish and French art collections are on this floor as well as on the second floor.

Nationalmuseet

Denmark's largest museum, the National Museum, presents the history and culture of the Danes from prehistoric times to the present. It also houses a wonderful collection of Greek and Egyptian antiquities, an ethnographic collection and the Children's Museum. Many of the displays derive from King Frederik III's Royal Cabinet of Curiosities, put together around 1650. The collection has been housed in the 18th-century Rococo Prince's Palace, overlooking Frederiksholms Kanal, since the 1850s.

The museum atrium

The Victorian Home, a plush apartment with authentic 19th-century interiors, owned by the museum, is located nearby *(see below)*.

Visit the museum café on the first floor for brunch or open sandwiches.

• Map J5
• Ny Vestergade 10
• 33 13 44 11
• Open 10am–5pm Tue–Sun • Free
• Free guided tours in English, Jun–Sep: 11am every Tue, Thu and Sun
• Call for details of activities in the Children's Museum
• Guided tours of the Victorian Home in English: Jun–Sep: 2pm every Sat (tickets are available from the information desk in the National Museum lobby); adm for adults 50 Dkr, concessions 40 Dkr, free for under-18s • www.natmus.dk

Top 10 Features

1. Sun Chariot
2. Oak Burial Coffins
3. Gundestrup Cauldron
4. State Rooms
5. Inuit Culture
6. China, Japan and the Far East
7. Prehistoric Denmark and the Viking Age
8. Room 117
9. Cylinder Perspective Table
10. Denmark's Oldest Coin

Key

▦ Ground floor
▦ First floor
▦ Second floor
▦ Third floor

Sun Chariot
The unique Sun Chariot or *Solvognen* *(right)*, a masterpiece of casting, was dug up in 1902 by a farmer ploughing his field. This 3,400-year-old artifact from the Bronze Age shows a horse on wheels pulling a large sun disk, gilded only on one side to represent its daytime trajectory.

Oak Burial Coffins
Seven Bronze-Age oak coffins, dating back to 1,400 BC, occupy space on the ground floor. The Egtved grave, holding the body of a well-preserved, fully clad young woman, is an extraordinary exhibit.

Gundestrup Cauldron
Found near Gundestrup, this silver cauldron *(right)* from the Iron Age, is decorated with animals and mystical figures.

State Rooms
The State Rooms date back to the time when this building was a royal palace. They are virtually intact from the period 1743–4; the Great Hall is adorned with the original Flemish tapestries.

Inuit Culture
5 This collection *(left)* from Greenland showcases the skill and creative ingenuity of the people of the frozen North. The displays include boats and clothing like embroidered anoraks and boots, assorted toys and watercolours of daily life.

China, Japan and the Far East
6 The Far East is well represented in this marvellous collection that includes Japanese laquerwork, fabulously costumed Samurai warriors, replete with weaponry, and beautiful 18th-century Imperial Dragon robes, worn by the Chinese emperor.

Prehistoric Denmark and the Viking Age
7 The museum's most popular exhibit is this comprehensive display of the country's 14,000-year history. These intricate golden horns *(right)*, reconstructed in the 20th century after the 400 BC originals were melted down in 1802, are a definite highlight.

Room 117
8 This 18th-century bourgeois interior can be traced to the town of Aalborg in Jutland. A wood-panelled room in a sea of glass-display galleries, it features a heavy wooden four-poster bed, chest, coffered wooden ceiling and mullioned windows.

Cylinder Perspective Table
9 In Room 126, this table is a part of Frederik III's Royal Cabinet of Curiosities. The table top shows him and his wife, Sophie Amalie, painted ingeniously in a distorted perspective: it gets rectified when viewed in the reflective surface of a cylinder at the centre of the table.

Denmark's Oldest Coin
10 The name of Denmark and an image of a Danish king were first depicted on this small silver coin *(left)* – displayed in Room 144 – that was struck in AD 995.

Museum Guide

Fronted by a courtyard, the museum's entrance hall has toilets and lockers. You can pick up a map and information in the atrium straight ahead. The museum shop, also located here, sells some interesting books and educational toys with a Viking twist. The Children's Museum *(see p56)* is to your left. If you are time-bound, opt for the 1-hour themed itineraries. The prehistoric collection is on the ground floor, while the first floor holds a range of collections, including one on ethnography. The second floor includes a History of Denmark collection (from 1660 to 2000). The antiquities are found on the third floor.

⓾ Slotsholmen

The small fishing village of Copenhagen was founded on the island of Slotsholmen in the 12th century. Bishop Absalon, the king's friend and supporter, built a castle here in 1167. Two centuries later, the castle was destroyed by the Hanseatic League, the European trade alliance, which resented Copenhagen's increasing control over trade. Christiansborg Palace, which stands here today, is home to the Danish Parliament, the Jewish Museum and the Palace Church.

Teatermuseet

This delightful court theatre, above the Royal Stables, was established in 1767. Now a museum, it depicts Danish theatre in the 18th and 19th centuries. The atmosphere is enhanced by classical music and displays of mannequins in court dresses. Visitors can also walk onto the stage.

Christiansborg Slotskirke

🍴 **Visit the restaurants on Gammel Strand and Højbro Plads.**

Top 10 Features

1. Christiansborg Slot
2. Ruins Under the Palace
3. Teatermuseet
4. Royal Stables
5. Royal Library Gardens
6. Tøjhusmuseet
7. Dansk Jødisk Museum
8. Christiansborg Slotskirke
9. Thorvaldsens Museum
10. Royal Reception Rooms

- Map J5
- *Christiansborg Slot: 33 92 64 92; open May–Sep: 10am–5pm daily; Oct–Apr: 10am–5pm Tue–Sun; guided tours in English of State Rooms May–Sep: 3pm daily; Oct–Apr: 3pm Tue–Sun; adm; www.christiansborg.dk*
- *Ruins: open May–Sep: 10am–5pm daily; Oct–Apr: 10am–5pm Tue–Sun; adm*
- *Royal Stables: 33 40 26 76; open May–Sep: 1:30–4pm daily; Oct–Apr: 1:30–4pm Tue–Sun; adm*
- *Royal Library Gardens: open all year*
- *Christiansborg Slotskirke: open 10am–5pm Sun; Jul: daily*
- *Tøjhusmuseet: 33 11 60 37; open noon–4pm Tue–Sun*
- *Thorvaldsens Museum: Bertel Thorvaldsens Plads 2; 33 32 15 32; open 10am–5pm Tue–Sun; adm, free Wednesdays; www.thorvaldsens museum.dk*

Christiansborg Slot

Designed in a Neo-Baroque style in 1907–28, this sturdy construction is built from reinforced concrete and granite-lined façades *(right)*. It houses the State Rooms, the Folketinget (the elected parliament), the Prime Minister's apartment and the High Court. The 106-m- (350-ft-) high tower is the tallest in the city.

Ruins Under the Palace

These fascinating ruins were discovered during the construction of the present palace. You can see parts of Bishop Absalon's castle and the second castle that stood here until the 18th century. You will also find interesting details of the routine of daily life, such as a baker's oven, latrine chutes and hollow tree trunks used as underground pipes.

Royal Stables

The stables *(below)* of Christian VI's Palace survived the fire of 1794. The Queen's horses are still kept here amid splendid marble walls, columns and mangers. There is also a collection of royal coaches and riding gear.

The ruins, Tøjhusmuseet and Thorvaldsens Museum all accept the Copenhagen Card, see p111.

5 Royal Library Gardens

Formerly a naval port, this oasis is tucked behind Christiansborg *(right)*. Designed in 1920, the fountains in the central pool cascade every hour. Check out the statue of philosopher Kierkegaard.

6 Tøjhusmuseet

Built as an arsenal by Christian IV in 1604–8, the Royal Danish Arsenal Museum is filled with artillery guns. The Armoury Hall on the first floor has 7,000 hand weapons, some from the 1300s.

7 Dansk Jødisk Museum

This museum *(below)* has a striking modern interior, designed by architect Daniel Libeskind. The small building brilliantly depicts the lives and culture of the Jewish population in Denmark *(see p34)*.

8 Christiansborg Slotskirke

Standing on the site of the original 18th-century church destroyed in the ferocious palace fire of 1794, this Neo-Classical church with warm yellow walls was built in 1813–26. However, a fire broke out in 1992 and destroyed its roof, dome and even parts of the interior. A service is held here every October for the opening of Parliament *(see also p41)*.

9 Thorvaldsens Museum

This museum is home to almost all of sculptor Bertel Thorvaldsen's works and some of his personal belongings. In the entrance hall are the original plaster casts of some of his most famous pieces. In 1848, his tomb was moved to the museum's courtyard.

10 Royal Reception Rooms

Christiansborg's State Rooms are used by Denmark's royal family for official functions. Enter the rooms via the Queen's Gate, the Guard's Room and the King's Stairway. Note the Throne Room, with its huge ceiling painting, and the Great Hall with 17 royal tapestries, which recount the history of Denmark and were presented to the Queen by Bjørn Nørgaard *(see p35)*.

Castle Island

Several castles have stood on this site through the centuries. The first one was built in 1167 by Bishop Absalon. A second castle, occupied by King Eric of Pomerania, was built in 1417. When the building was beginning to fall apart, it was demolished in 1731 by Christian VI. In its place, he built a Baroque palace he considered suitable for an Absolute Monarch. It was completed in 1745, but was destroyed in the fire of 1794. Another castle was built in 1803–28, but also burned down in 1884. Finally, the present castle was built in 1907–28.

For full details and opening times of the Teatermuseet and Dansk Jødisk Museum, **see pp34–5**.

Detail from a painting showing the destruction of the Danish navy, 1801

🔟 Moments in History

1 Bishop Absalon's Castle

Originally a fishing village called Havn, Copenhagen was founded around AD 1000 on the island of Slotsholmen *(see pp28–9)* and prospered greatly from the shoals of herring that appeared in its waters. In the 1160s it was given by Valdemar I to his adviser, Bishop Absalon, who built a castle here as protection against raiders. The prosperity of Havn became a threat to the Hanseatic League, an alliance of trading guilds that monopolized trade in Northern Europe. They repeatedly attacked the castle, finally destroying it in 1367.

Søren Kierkegaard

2 Copenhagen, Capital of Denmark

King Erik VII took up residence in the second castle in 1416, by which time Havn, now Kjøbmande-havn (Merchants' Harbour), was a major economic centre. It was proclaimed as the capital of Denmark in 1443.

3 Civil War and the Reformation

Between 1534 and 1536, the Protestant king, Christian III, successfully withstood an uprising against him in favour of his Catholic cousin, Christian II. Christian III brought about the Reformation in Denmark.

4 The Founding of the University of Copenhagen

King Christian I inaugurated the University of Copenhagen on 1 June 1479. The university consisted of four faculties: Theology, Law, Medicine and Philosophy, and like all universities of the time was part of the Roman Catholic Church.

5 Absolute Monarchy

In 1660, Frederik III introduced Absolute Monarchy, enhancing the powers of the middle classes. Frederik VII abolished it in 1848 in favour of an elected parliament.

6 Wars with Sweden

Sharing the Sound meant the Swedes and Danes were in constant dispute. In the winter of 1657, the Swedes crossed the frozen Sound on foot, attacking Copenhagen. The ensuing Treaty of Roskilde saw Denmark cede its Swedish territories.

Bombardment of Copenhagen, 1807

Preceding pages: **Interior of the Marmorkirken dome.**

Ceremony introducing Absolute Monarchy

The Great Plague
7 Between June 1711 and March 1712, Copenhagen was hit by bubonic plague, wiping out 20,000 of its 60,000 inhabitants. It is said to have been brought in by ships from Sweden or East Prussia, carrying infected vermin.

The Fire of 1728
8 In the month of October, within four days, the greatest fire in Copenhagen's history wiped out almost all of northern Copenhagen. It began early in the morning at Vester Kvarter 146 – now roughly at the top of Strøget. Five churches, the university library, and 1,600 houses were destroyed.

The Battles of Copenhagen
9 Early in the 19th century, the city suffered more lasting damage when the British attacked in 1801, destroying the Danish navy, and again in 1807 to discourage the Danes from supporting France in the Napoleonic wars.

Rescue of the Danish Jews
10 The Nazis occupied Denmark during World War II from 1940 to 1945. In 1943, when the Jews were ordered to be deported to Germany, a collective of Danes and Swedes secretly evacuated virtually the entire Jewish population to Sweden by sea. As a result, most Danish Jews survived the war.

Top 10 Historical Figures

1 Harald Bluetooth (911–987)
King Harald converted Denmark to Christianity.

2 King Cnut (994/5–1035)
Ruled England, Norway and Denmark for 20 years and famously failed to hold back the waves.

3 Bishop Absalon (1128–1201)
Counsellor to King Valdemar I, he built the first castle on Slotsholmen.

4 Christian IV (1577–1648)
Christian promoted shipping and overseas trade and built the Rundetårn and Rosenborg Palace.

5 Tycho Brahe (1546–1601)
Brahe's astronomical tables were used to plot the rules of planetary motion.

6 Vitus Jonasson Bering (1681–1741)
A Danish explorer who discovered the Bering Strait, Sea, Island and Land Bridge.

7 Hans Christian Ørsted (1777–1851)
Danish physicist who discovered electromagnetism.

8 Søren Kierkegaard (1813–55)
A Danish philosopher, who first put forward the theory of "existentialism".

9 Knud Rasmussen (1879–1933)
The first man to cross the Northwest Passage by dogsled.

10 Niels Bohr (1885–1962)
A Nobel prize-winner (1922), Bohr contributed vastly to the understanding of quantum mechanics.

Left **Teatermuseet** Centre **Designmuseum Danmark** Right **Thorvaldsens Museum**

🔟 Museums and Galleries

Ny Carlsberg Glyptotek

This museum houses a fabulous collection of antiquities from Egypt, Greece, Rome and the Mediterranean coast. You will also find an impressive collection of 19th- and early 20th-century Danish and French fine arts, including Impressionist and Post-Impressionist collections *(see pp24–5)*.

Egyptian statues at Ny Carlsberg Glyptotek

Nationalmuseet

At Denmark's largest museum of cultural history you can explore the history of the Danes right up to the present day. Artifacts range from Iron Age burials and Renaissance interiors to African masks and houses on stilts. Check out the museum's spectacular ethnographic collection, including the world's oldest painting by South American Indians *(see pp26–7)*.

Viking culture at the Nationalmuseet

Statens Museum for Kunst

Nestled in a park with lakes and grassy slopes, the National Gallery displays a large collection of international art, with works by Great Masters like Dürer and Titian and by modern icons such as Picasso and Matisse. These are displayed side by side with 20th-century Danish works, including those of the controversial CoBrA group *(see pp22–3)*.

Dansk Jødisk Museum

The Danish Jewish Museum tells the story of Denmark's Jewish community since the arrival of the first families in the 17th century. Designed by architect Daniel Libeskind, the interlocking interior symbolizes Danish–Jewish good relations, its apogee the rescue of 7,000 Jews from the Nazis. ⊗ *Map K5*
• *Proviant-passangen 6* • *33 11 22 18*
• *Open Sep–May: 1pm–4pm Tue–Fri, noon–5pm Sat–Sun; Jun–Aug: 10am–5pm Tue–Sun* • *Adm for adults; free with Copenhagen Card* • *www.jewmus.dk*

Davids Samling

Set inside a 19th-century town house, the museum holds the collections of Christian Ludwig David (1878–1960), a Danish barrister. It includes fabulous furniture from the 18th–20th centuries and ancient Islamic ornamental art *(see p76)*.

Teatermuseet
On display are sections including the stage, the auditorium and dressing rooms of the 18th-century Royal Theatre (see p19) that survived the fire of 1794.

⊛ Map J5 • Christiansborg Ridebane 18 • 33 11 51 76 • Open 11am–3pm Tue–Thu, 1–4pm Sat–Sun • Adm for adults; free with Copenhagen Card • www. teatermuseet.dk

Frihedsmuseet
The Danish Resistance Museum explores Danish life during the Nazi occupation during 1940–45. The museum is currently closed due to extensive fire damage (see p77).

Designmuseum Danmark
One half of the Danish Museum of Decorative Art holds a collection of Chinese and Japanese artifacts, along with European medieval and Rococo arts. The other half is dedicated to cutting-edge Danish 20th- and 21st-century design. English labelling is limited (see p77).

Thorvaldsens Museum
Opened in 1848, this museum pays homage to the Neo-Classical sculptor Bertel Thorvaldsen. It includes most of his works, as well as some private belongings. You can also visit his grave, transferred here from Vor Frue Kirke in 1848, four years after his demise (see pp28–9).

Den Hirschsprungske Samling
Housed in a villa across the lake from the Statens Museum for Kunst, this art museum features a collection of late-19th- and early 20th-century Danish art – notably the Skagen school, Denmark's equally appealing answer to the Impressionists (see p75).

Top 10 Danish Artists

1 Bertel Thorvaldsen (1770–1844)
Son of an Icelandic wood carver, he became Denmark's most famous sculptor.

2 Christoffer Eckersberg (1783–1853)
Laid the foundations for the "Golden Age of Painting" in Denmark (1800–1850).

3 Michael Ancher (1849–1927)
One of the best-known artists in Denmark and the unofficial head of the Skagen group.

4 Peder Severin Krøyer (1851–1909)
His work is inspired by the lives of the fishermen of Skagen.

5 Anna Ancher (1859–1935)
A Skagen artist and wife of Michael Ancher. Her work is typified by picturesque, intimate scenes of family life.

6 Vilhelm Hammershøi (1864–1916)
Known for his paintings of interiors, done in muted colours.

7 Richard Mortensen (1910–1993)
The first Danish artist to turn to abstraction. Also known for his perfect technical finish.

8 Asger Jorn (1914–73)
Founder of CoBrA, an important art group to emerge after World War II.

9 Bjørn Nørgaard (1947–)
One of the most influential Danish contemporary artists, his works span a range of fields, including sculpture. He also designed the Queen's Tapestries.

10 Olafur Eliasson (1967–)
Danish–Icelandic artist who erects fascinating kinetic sculptures inspired by natural phenomena in cities worldwide.

Copenhagen's Top 10

Left **Rosenborg Slot** Centre **Den Sorte Diamant** Right **Christiansborg Slot**

🔟 Historic Buildings

1 Rosenborg Slot

This lovely, turreted Renaissance castle was built by Christian IV. Now a royal museum, its collections and interior provide a vivid picture of the monarchy over the centuries. The crown jewels are on display in the basement (see pp14–15).

Chapel Portal at Frederiksborg Slot

2 Christiansborg Slot

This Neo-Baroque palace, built in the early 20th century, is the seat of the government and the fourth palace on the site. Visit the 12th–14th-century ruins of the first two castles built here, the 18th-century theatre and stables and the State Rooms (see p28).

3 Rundetårn

This curious Round Tower was built by Christian IV and affords a wonderful view over the old town. It also has a gallery that holds innovative, changing exhibitions (see p16).

4 Børsen

The stock exchange is remarkable for its tower with a striking spire designed to look like four entwined dragons' tails. The three crowns at the top of the building represent the kingdoms of Denmark, Sweden and Norway. ◎ Map K5 • Børsgade • Not open to the public

5 Frederiksborg Slot

This beautiful, grand Renaissance castle is a short train ride out of Copenhagen. Christian IV was living here when he fell seri-ously ill and demanded to be taken to his favourite palace, Rosenborg, for his last few days. Don't miss the castle's ornate chapel (see pp98–9).

6 Regensen

Built by Christian IV in the 17th century as a student hostel, Regensen still retains that function today. Unfortunately, most of the building was burnt down in the city fire of 1728 (see p33), but so vital was it to the life of the university that it was rebuilt shortly after (see p17).

7 Radisson Blu Royal Hotel

A 1950s icon or a horrible tower block? Designed by architect Arne Jacobsen (see p39), this hotel underwent a makeover in the 1980s; the original interior was retained only in Room 606. If it is unoccupied and you ask nicely, they might let you have a look at the room. The foyer has a 1960s retro cool look and includes Jacobsen's interesting Swan and Egg chairs. You can enjoy excellent views of the city from the restaurant (see p83).

For more historic churches, see pp40–41.

Holmens Kirke

The only Renaissance church in Copenhagen was built as a sailors' forge in 1562–3 and converted into a naval church by Christian IV in 1619. The exotic font is the work of a local 17th-century blacksmith. The metal fence shows golden elephants carrying black castles on their backs, a depiction of the royal Danish elephant. ◈ *Map K5 • Holmens Kanal • 33 13 61 78 • Open 10am–4pm Mon, Wed, Fri & Sat, 10am–3:30pm Tue & Thu, noon–4pm Sun & public holidays*

Den Sorte Diamant

The Black Diamond, a modern extension of the Royal Library, was built by architects Schmidt, Hammer and Lassen. It houses the National Museum of Photography, the Queen's Hall concert space, an exhibition area and Søren K, a smart restaurant. The shiny tiled exterior is highly reflective and a favourite photo opportunity for the boat-trippers floating past *(see p8)*.

Operaen

The remarkable Opera House stands on the banks of the Holmen, formerly Copenhagen's naval dockyard. The auditorium is a masterpiece of acoustic design, from the velour seats that do not absorb sound to the distance between the front of the stage and the back wall, which allows for the perfect time to achieve greatest clarity. Over 100,000 pieces of 23.75 carat gold leaf make up the ceiling *(see p91)*.

Operaen

Top 10 Statues

The Little Mermaid
The city's icon, inspired by the fairy tale. ◈ *Langelinie, top end of Kastellet*

Gefionspringvandet
Statue depicting the fable of the goddess Gefion and the king of Denmark. ◈ *Langelinie, by St Alban's Church*

Fiskerkone
The *Fishwife* was created in 1940 and installed at the spot where fish have been sold since the medieval times. ◈ *Gammel Strand*

Lurblæserne
It is said that the *Hornblowers* will sound the Viking horns whenever a virgin passes by – no one has heard a peep out of them yet. ◈ *Rådhuspladsen*

Frederik V
Sculptor Jacques Saly took 18 years to finish this statue. Unveiled in 1771, it merited a 27-gun salute. ◈ *Amalienborg Slotsplads*

Christian V
This shows the king dressed as a Roman emperor riding over a fallen figure. ◈ *Kongens Nytorv*

Hans Christian Andersen
Famous sculpture by Henry Lukow-Nielsen. ◈ *Corner of Rådhus, H C Andersens Boulevard*

Hans Christian Andersen
Includes scenes from his fairy tales. ◈ *Kongens Have*

Caritas Springvandet
One of the oldest statues in Copenhagen, dating back to 1608. ◈ *Gammel Torv*

The Elephant Gate
Big, splendid elephants at the Carlsberg Brewery gateway. ◈ *Gammel Carlsberg Vej 11*

At the end of university exams in the spring, it is traditional for Copenhagen's students to dance around the statue of Christian V.

Left **Vor Frue Kirke** Centre **Hotel d'Angleterre** Right **Nyhavn**

Hans Christian Andersen Sights

Det Kongelige Teater
Hans Christian Andersen arrived in Copenhagen on 6 September 1819 as a star-struck 14-year-old. It was "my second birthday", he recounts in his biography, *The Fairytale of My Life*. Determined to become an actor, he went straight to the Royal Theatre in search of a job. Although occasionally employed as an actor, his acting talent never quite matched his skill as a writer *(see pp18–19)*.

Bakkehusmuseet
The Bakkehus (House on the Hill) was the home of prominent literary patron Knud Rahbek and his wife, Kamma Lyhne Rahbek, from 1802 to 1830. Andersen met the couple in the early 1820s and their home soon became a meeting place for poets and authors. The museum retains a homely atmosphere and recreates the Golden Age of creativity. It also includes various mementos that belonged to Andersen *(see pp84–5)*.

Vingårdsstræde 6
Andersen lived here for a year in 1827 in a spartan garret room (then No 132), preparing for his university exams. This is where he wrote the sad poem *The Student*. Once a museum, the room is no longer open to the public.

Nyhavn Nos 18, 20 and 67
Andersen lived in lodgings on Nyhavn for much of his life, including at Nyhavn 280 (now No 20) in 1834, No 67 in 1848 and No 18 (a private hotel) in 1871. He lived here until 1875, when he fell terminally ill and moved in with the Melchiors, who nursed him in their own home *(see p18)*.

Magasin du Nord
In 1838, Andersen moved into Hotel du Nord, now the department store Magasin du Nord. Here he rented two rooms in the attic, one of which overlooked the Royal Theatre. The next-door Mini's Café became a regular haunt for the writer *(see pp18–19)*.

Rundetårn
The exhibition space here was once the university library where Andersen spent many hours. His first fairy tale, *The Tinderbox* (1835), talks of a dog with eyes "as big as a tower" guarding a treasure. Scholars

Department store Magasin (once Hotel) du Nord

See also the Wonderful World of HC Andersen Museum on **pp56 and 66**

Rundetårn's cobbled spiral ramp

believe this refers to the Rundetårn, which was built as an observatory – a literal eye to the sky *(see p16)*.

Hotel d'Angleterre

Andersen stayed here in November 1860, when he occupied two rooms at the corner of Kongens Nytorv and Østergade (Strøget), close to the Royal Theatre; between August 1869 and March 1870; and finally, during April–May 1871 *(see p112)*.

Lille Kongensgade 1

In October 1866, Andersen took a suite of rooms on the third floor, rented out by a photographer, Thora Hallager. Here, he bought furniture for the first time in his life (at the age of 61), as this was an unfurnished apartment. ✎ *Map K4*

Vor Frue Kirke

Andersen died on 4 August 1875 of liver cancer. His funeral, a national event attended by the king and crown prince, was held at Vor Frue Kirke in the Old Town *(see p17)*.

Assistens Kirkegård

This is the cemetery where Andersen's body was interred in Nørrebro. The stone is inscribed with inspirational lines from his poem "Oldingen" or "The Old Man" (1874) *(see p75)*.

Top 10 Danish Cultural Figures

1 August Bournonville (1805–1879)
Choreographer and ballet master who created many works for the Danish ballet.

2 Carl Nielsen (1865–1931)
Composer, violinist and pianist. Best known for his symphonies and the operas *Saul og David* and *Maskerade*.

3 Karen Blixen (1885–1962)
Her famous novel, *Out of Africa (1937)*, was published under the pen name Isak Dinesen.

4 Poul Henningsen (1894–1967)
Architect, author and anti-traditionalist. Best known for his PH lamps *(see p47)*.

5 Arne Jacobsen (1902–1971)
Architect and designer who defined the concept of Danish design – fluid and practical.

6 Lars von Trier (1956–)
Film director famous for the Dogme95 Collective and his technique of cinematic minimalism.

7 Viggo Mortensen (1958–)
Popular as Aragorn in *The Lord of the Rings* films.

8 Mads Mikkelsen (1965–)
Made his international acting breakthrough as Bond villain Le Chiffre in *Casino Royale*.

9 Helena Christensen (1968–)
Miss Denmark (1986) and a Supermodel of the 1990s.

10 Sofie Gråbøl (1968–)
Played detective Sarah Lund in hit crime series *Forbrydelsen (The Killing)*.

Left **Christians Kirke** Centre **Marmorkirken** Right **Sankt Petri Kirke**

🔟 Churches

Helligåndskirken
Dating back to the 12th century, these are among the oldest architectural remains in Copenhagen. Only Helligånds-huset (now used for markets and exhibitions), Christian IV's Baroque portal and Griffenfeld's Chapel survive. Much of the original church burnt down in the fire of 1728. The church re-opened after reconstruction in 1732 *(see p16)*.

Christians Kirke
This church was built in the Rococo style in 1755–9 by Nicolai Eigtved, Frederik V's master architect. It is starkly different from most Danish churches: in-stead of the congregation sitting only in pews in the nave, the church has a second gallery level (like that of a theatre) where all the important worshippers were seated *(see p89)*.

Vor Frelsers Kirke
This splendid Baroque church was built in 1682–96 at the behest of Christian V. The king's royal insignia can be seen at various places in the church, including on the organ case, which is supported by elephants, the symbol of Denmark's prestigious Order of the Elephant. The spire is 90 m (295 ft) high, and the tower affords a magnificent view of the city. The interior of the church is bright and well lit, thanks to the white walls and tall windows *(see p89)*.

Trinitatis Kirke
Standing next door to the Rundetårn is the Trinitatis Kirke. Commissioned by Christian IV in 1637, this lovely church was completed in the reign of Frederik III in 1656. The present interior dates back to 1731, as the original was burnt in the fire of 1728. It includes boxed pews with seashell carvings, a gilded altar-piece, a Baroque dark wood pulpit and a fabulous gold-and-silver coloured organ *(see pp16–17)*.

Vor Frue Kirke
Also known as St Mary's Cathedral, the church has been on this site in different forms since the 12th century and has played host to royal and national events over the years. It has a 19th-century façade and a bright interior dominated by statues of Christ and his Apostles *(see pp16–17)*.

Holmens Kirke

6 Sankt Petri Kirke

This is the city's oldest church. Unlike most medieval buildings, it survived the fire of 1728. Its tower, nave and choir date back to the 15th century. The north and south transepts were added in 1634 (see pp16–17).

7 Holmens Kirke

Originally built in 1562 as a naval forge, it was converted into a church in 1619. The Baroque altarpiece is fantastically ornate, and the pulpit is the tallest in Denmark (see p37).

8 Marmorkirken

This circular church has an imposing presence. The dome's interior is covered with paintings of the 12 Apostles and light floods in from 12 skylights. Originally designed by Nicolai Eigtved in 1740, work on the building was suspended in 1770, due to increasing expenses, and began again after nearly 150 years, financed by Carl Frederik Tietgen and redesigned by Ferdinand Meldahl. It was inaugurated on 19 August 1894 (see pp20–21).

9 Grundtvigs Kirke

This suburban parish church was built in the 1920s–30s by P V Jensen Klint and his son, Kaare Klint (see p47). It has yellow-brick walls and an impressive modern Gothic appearance. To visit, take the train to Emdrup.
Ⓢ På Bjerget 14B, Bispebjerg • 35 81 54 42 • Open 9am–4pm Mon–Sat, noon–4pm Sun (to 1pm Nov–Apr) • www.grundtvigskirke.dk

Grundtvigs Kirke

10 Christiansborg Slotskirke

The original 18th-century Rococo creation was destroyed in the palace fire of 1794 and was rebuilt in a Neo-Classical style with a central dome. Inaugurated on Whit Sunday in 1826 to mark the 1,000th anniversary of Christianity in Denmark, it succumbed to another fire in 1992, but has now been rebuilt (see pp28–9).

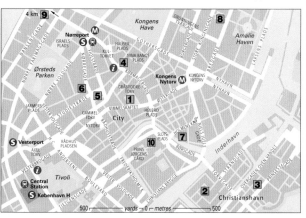

Further afield, don't miss Roskilde's Gothic brick cathedral which doubles as a mausoleum for the Danish royal family, see p100.

Left **Det Kongelige Teater** Right **Jazzhouse**

Performing Arts and Music Venues

Operaen

Operaen
Famed for its acoustics, the Opera House attracts a variety of international productions. You can enjoy a good view of the stage from any seat and all the seats are relatively cheap due to government subsidy *(see p91)*.

Det Kongelige Teater
This is a great destination for a night of entertainment. World-class performances of ballet are held on the old stage in Kongens Nytorv *(see pp18–19)*, while dramatic works are performed at the playhouse on the waterfront, Skuespilhuset.

Jazzhouse
Copenhagen's biggest venue for jazz, the Jazzhouse offers a varied programme of both Danish and international musicians. On weekends, late night concerts kick off at 11pm. ✆ Map J4 • Niels Hemmingsens Gade 10 • 33 15 37 00 • www.jazzhouse.dk

Mojo Bluesbar
Smoky, small, dark and intimate, this bar is known for its laid-back blues and live jazz performances. There won't be any distracting gimmicks or performance technology on display here. It is very popular, so book ahead. ✆ Map H5 • Løngangs-træde 21C • 33 11 64 53 • www.mojo.dk

Wallmans Cirkusbygningen
This circular former circus building (1884) is now a glamorous venue offering old-fashioned "dinner, show and dancing". There is surround-entertainment on seven stages while resting members of the cast serve you a good dinner. After the show, it turns into a nightclub. ✆ Map G5 • Cirkusbyningen, Jernbanegade 8 • 33 16 37 00 • www.wallmans.dk

Tivoli Concert Hall
The Tivoli Concert Hall is the city's largest music venue, with a capacity of 1,900. It stages over 100 operas, ballets, rock and jazz concerts during the Tivoli season *(see pp11–12)*.

Mojo Bluesbar

Tivoli Concert Hall

Det Ny Teater

This early 20th-century theatre hosts popular international musicals, such as *Phantom of the Opera* and *Les Misérables*. ⊗ *Map C5 • Gammel Kongevej 29 • 33 25 50 75 • www.detnyteater.dk*

Koncerthuset

The concert house of national broadcaster Danmarks Radio (DR) was designed by Jean Nouvel. Located in DR-Byen (broadcasting city) in the Ørestad district, this landmark building with its blue glass façade has superior acoustics. ⊗ *Map B3 • Ørestads Boulevard 13 • 35 20 62 62 • www.dr.dk/ koncerthuset*

Parken

This football stadium held its first indoor concert in 2001 with the Eurovision Song Concert. Famous bands including U2, Metallica and Madonna have performed here since. ⊗ *Map D2*

VEGA

Occupying a 1950s trade union building, VEGA offers club nights that attract international acts and DJs. The venue is also used regularly for concerts. ⊗ *Map B6 • Enghavevej 40 • 33 25 70 11 • Club nights 11pm–4am Fri–Sat; adm: 60 Dkr after 1am • www.vega.dk*

Top 10 Jazz Venues and Events

Bars and Cafés
Popular places include Christianshavn's Sofiekælderen *(see p93)* and Nørrebro's Café Blågårds Apotek.

Charlie Scott's
Tiny city-centre bar enjoyed by hardened jazz lovers. ⊗ *Skindergade 43 • 33 12 12 20*

Jazzhus Montmartre
This legendary venue seats just 70 people. ⊗ *Store Renegade 19a • 31 72 34 94*

La Fontaine
Known for late sessions, from 11pm Fri–Sat. ⊗ *Kompagnistræde 11 • 33 11 60 98*

Huset-KBH
This city council-funded culture house hosts a regular jazz club on the first floor. ⊗ *Rådhusstræde 13 • 21 51 21 51*

Jazzcup
Both a record store and a café hosting experimental jazz sessions on weekend afternoons. ⊗ *Gothersgade 107 • 33 15 02 02*

The Standard
Art Deco building on the waterfront with shows daily (except Mon) on the first floor. ⊗ *Havnegade 44 • 72 14 88 08*

Tango y Vinos
Tiny Argentinian wine bar hosting musicians on weekends. Jazz, flamenco, funk and tango. ⊗ *Herluf Trolles Gade 9 • 33 32 81 16*

Copenhagen Jazz Festival
For 10 days in July, jazz spills out into the streets, squares and historic buildings.

Winter Jazz
An extension of the jazz festival, this smaller programme takes place in Jan–Feb.

Left **A brunch café in Halmtorvet** Right **Cyclists relaxing by Rosenborg Slot**

Outdoor Activities

A canal tour

Bikes
Almost every major road in Copenhagen has a cycle lane and you can hire a bike *(see p106)* for a day or more. In summer, you can hop onto a free City Bike and ride within city limits. There are 2000 City Bikes available to rent for a refundable fee; some have built-in touch screens and GPS.

Canal tours
Canal and harbour trips are a lovely way to see the city. There are two canal tour companies *(see p8)*; both begin trips at Nyhavn. You can also tour the city on a harbour bus *(see p8)*. If you are carrying a Copenhagen Card *(see p111)*, you can change buses using just a single ticket.

Outdoor Dining
In the 1990s, Copenhagen witnessed a surge in outdoor dining venues. Now, virtually all cafés and restaurants offer outdoor dining in the summer. Blankets and heaters are provided for when it gets chilly. Nyhavn and Peblinge Dossering offer particularly good views.

Flea Markets
There are many outdoor flea markets in the summer, offering everything from furniture and clothing to pseudo-antiques and retro vinyl.
○ *Frederiksberg Rådhusplads: Map A5; Apr–Oct: 8am–3pm Sat • Bertel Thorvaldsens Plads: Map J5; May–Sep: 8am–5pm Fri, 9am–5pm Sat • Ravnsborggade, Nørrebro: Map D3; Mar–Nov: 10am–4pm Sun*

Tivoli
At Tivoli, you can wander through the stalls, check out the rides, listen to the Tivoli bands (free rock and pop concerts on Friday nights), or simply relax on a lakeside bench *(see pp10–11)*.

Lounging by the Lakes
Man-made lakes divide the main city from Nørrebro and Østerbro. Of these, Skt Jørgens

Copenhagen flea market

Zoologisk Have

Sø, Peblinge Sø and Sortedams Sø are easily accessible. You can lounge along their grassy banks or enjoy the scenic view from the bridges that cross them.

Dyrehaven

This deer park (it does still have lots of deer – the rutting season is in the autumn), has been here since the 16th century. It is like an English park or common and features a noisy, enjoyable funfair, called Bakken. For a bit of excitement, take a pony-and-trap ride. ⚄ Map B2 • Dyrehaven Klampenborg • www.bakken.dk

Kongens Have

Attached to Rosenborg Slot, the King's Garden is a great place to sunbathe, play frisbee, cricket or football, or have a picnic. In the summer, you can catch a puppet show or a jazz concert (see pp14–15).

Assistens Kirkegård

This beautiful, meandering churchyard holds the graves of famous Danes like Hans Christian Andersen, August Bournonville and Niels Bohr (see p75).

Zoologisk Have

You will find polar bears, lions, tigers, elephants and other animals in this delightful zoo. There are thematic adventure trails for kids (see p83).

Top 10 Beaches and Pools

Havnebadet
Popular floating harbour pool with fresh water. ⚄ Islands Brygge • 23 71 31 89

Bellevue
Full of people playing, sailing or relaxing. Left end is nudist. ⚄ Strandvejen 340, 2930 Klampenborg

Fælledparkens Soppesø
Huge, child-friendly, outdoor pool. ⚄ Borgmester Jensens Allé 50, Østerbro • 33 66 36 60

Amager Strandpark
Luxury Beach with lagoon, artificial island and snack kiosks. ⚄ Amager Strandvej • www.amager-strand.dk

Køge Bugt Strandpark
A 7-km (4-mile) beach along Køge Bay from Brøndby to Hundige. ⚄ Ishøj Store Torv 20, 2635 Ishøj

Bellahøj Svømmestadion
Indoor and outdoor swimming facilities, including water slides. ⚄ Bellahøjvej 1–3, Brønshøj • 38 26 21 40

Frederiksdal Friluftsbad
Gorgeous lakeside beach with café. ⚄ Frederiksdal Badesti 1, Virum • 45 83 81 85

DGI-Byen
Indoor facilities with a "super-ellipse" pool and a kids' pool. ⚄ Corner of Tietgensgade & Ingerslevsgade • 33 29 81 40

Charlottenlund Beach
Good place for sunbathing. ⚄ Park Strandvejen 144, Charlottenlund

Copencabana Havne-badet ved Fisketorvet
Includes a floating harbour pool and three outdoor pools. ⚄ Havneholmen 0, Vesterbro • 27 52 90 28

For more outdoor activities beyond Copenhagen, **see pp96–102.**

Left **Girlie Hurley, Vesterbro** Centre **Shopping street, Strøget (north)** Right **Shop front, Bredgade**

Shopping Districts

Strøget
Copenhagen's shopping street is known by many simply as "the walking street". The shops, which stretch across five linked pedestrian streets, range from cheerful and inexpensive outlets to designer and up-market department stores (towards Kongens Nytorv). It has something for everyone, from bargain clothes to exclusive silver, porcelain and glassware in the Royal Scandinavia shops. Strøget is also popular for its street performers. ✆ *Map H5–K4*

Off Strøget (North)
Heading up north from Strøget, you will find numerous little boutiques, record stores and second-hand shops. Indulge in some individual shopping on streets like Skindergade, Larsbjørnstræde, Vestergade, Studiestræde and Sankt Peders Stræde. ✆ *Map H4–J4*

Strøget

Glam clothes shop in Nørrebro

Off Strøget (South)
The streets to the south of Strøget are great for "alternative" shopping. Læderstræde and Kompagnistræde are especially good, the latter mostly for its antique shops. ✆ *Map J4–J5*

Kronprinsensgade
This posh shopping area includes many of Scandinavia's top designer brands, such as Stig P and Le-Fix. You will also find Scandinavia's oldest tea shop, Perch's Tea Room. ✆ *Map J4*

Nansensgade
Located on the outskirts of the old town, this area has a mix of traditional and trendy boutiques, as well as good restaurants and cafés. ✆ *Map G3*

Nørrebro
Not as trendy as it once was, but still with many second-hand stores and chic boutiques. Check out Ravnsborggade for antique finds, Jaegersborggade for the offbeat and Elmegade for vintage clothes. ✆ *Map C3–D3*

For more shopping alternatives, see pp80, 86, 92.

7 Vesterbro

This former red-light area is now an offbeat shopping district offering good bargains. Among the more interesting streets are Istedgade, which is lined with boutiques and art shops, and Værnedamsvej, which has several independent fashion stores and gourmet food shops. ⊗ Map C5–C6

8 Torvehallerne Kbh

Food-lovers are in for a treat at Copenhagen's covered market on Israels Plads, with gourmet food stands, takeout delights and delicious delis. ⊗ Map H3

9 Fisketorv Shopping Centre

Situated on the waterfront facing the Inner Harbour, this city mall is a few minutes away from the Copencabana harbour pool (see p45). It has more than 120 shops, several restaurants and a multiplex cinema. ⊗ Map J6
• Kalvebod Brygge 59, Vesterbro • 35 37 19 17 • Open 10am–8pm Mon–Fri, 10am–6pm Sat–Sun

10 Bredgade

If you are looking for traditional, pre-20th-century antiques, this is the perfect place to visit. Here you will find several grand-looking shops and auction houses that sell all kinds of antiques, including authentic paintings and statues. ⊗ Map L3

Kronprinsensgade

Top 10 Danish Design Companies

1 Kjærholm Furniture
Poul Kjærholm-designed functional coffee tables and chairs, all named simply PK with a number. Production continues under the leadership of his son, Thomas.

2 Cylinda-Line (by Arne Jacobsen)
Popular tableware collection (1967) in steel, wood and plastic. ⊗ www.stelton.dk

3 Bang & Olufsen
Known for their cutting-edge audio-visual designs. ⊗ www.bang-olufsen.com

4 Kaare Klint Furniture
Combines ergonomics with elegant 18th-century English styles.

5 Bodum
Classic and smart kitchenware in steel and glass. ⊗ www.bodum.com

6 LEGO®
These popular building blocks were introduced in 1952. ⊗ www.lego.com

7 Vipp
Designers of a classic stainless steel pedal bin, Vipp's products also include soap dishes and dispensers. ⊗ www.vipp.com

8 Flora Danica Porcelain
Royal porcelain design featuring floral motifs. ⊗ www.royalcopenhagen.com

9 Poul Henningsen Lamps
Famous lamp design, creating the effect of maximum light and minimum shadow.

10 Georg Jensen Silverware
Original, organic tableware designs and casual jewellery. ⊗ www.georgjensen.com

Left **Formel B** Right **Le Sommelier**

Restaurants

Grønbech & Churchill
Award-winning chef Rasmus Grønbech is known for his imaginative dishes that combine classic cooking with ingenious taste combinations. The set four-course menu is reasonably priced considering that the restaurant has a Michelin star. ◊ Map L2 • Esplanaden 48 • 32 21 32 30 • Open noon–2:30pm and 6–10pm Mon–Fri, 6–10pm Sat
• www.gronbech-churchill.dk
• ⓀⓀⓀⓀⓀ

Umami
While the slick, contemporary design and attentive service here are noteworthy, it is the food that stands out. The delicate flavours that arise from combining Japanese and French cuisines have to be experienced to be believed. ◊ Map K3 • Store Kongensgade 59 • 33 38 75 00
• Open 6–10pm Mon–Thu, 6–11pm Fri–Sat
• www.restaurantumami.dk • ⓀⓀⓀⓀⓀ

Frikadeller

Kong Hans Kælder
This unique restaurant has whitewashed, underlit arches in Copenhagen's oldest building. Watch the chef in the open kitchen as he cooks up fancy dishes from the à la carte and fixed-price menus. ◊ Map K4
• Vingårdsstræde 6 • 33 11 68 68 • Open 6pm–midnight Mon–Sat (kitchen closes at 10pm) • www.konghans.dk • ⓀⓀⓀⓀⓀ

AOC
Dine with class in the romantic and elegant surroundings of the 18th-century Moltkes Palace basement. AOC's name stands for Aarø & Co, after sommelier and owner Christian Aarø. The inventive set courses are perfectly presented and have earned the restaurant a Michelin star. ◊ Map K3 • Dronningens Tværgade 2 • 33 11 11 45 • Open 6pm–1am Tue–Sat
• www.restaurantaoc.dk • ⓀⓀⓀⓀⓀ

Era Ora
Umbrian cuisine is served in this well-established Italian restaurant. Enjoy lunchtime alfresco dining or fuller evening menus (of 12–17 small dishes) in this 18th-century building's warmly decorated room. Combined food and wine lists are also available for up to 3,800 Dkr (see p93).

Godt
The modest blue-painted exterior conceals a fabulous dining experience at this appropriately named ("good") restaurant. The English chef regularly wanders around the 20-seater restaurant adding that personal touch to this husband-and-wife enterprise. ◊ Map K3
• Gothersgade 38 • 33 15 21 22
• Open 6pm–midnight Tue–Sat
• www.restaurant-godt.dk • ⓀⓀⓀⓀⓀ

For more restaurants and a key to price categories, see pp67, 71, 79, 87, 93 and 103.

Noma

7 Voted the world's best restaurant at the San Pellegrino awards three years in a row, Noma offers superior Nordic fare sourced from Denmark, Iceland, Greenland and the Faroe Islands. Run by chef René Redzepi, the restaurant is housed in a fabulous warehouse dating from 1767. The interior has a shabby-chic look with open beams. It is Denmark's only 2-Michelin-starred restaurant *(see p93)*.

Le Sommelier

8 A first-rate French restaurant, with impeccable staff, a pleasant atmosphere and a massive wine list. The *foie gras* is delicious. In the right season, be sure to try the seafood. The chocolate plate laden with five different chocolate-inspired confections is hard to resist. ○ *Map L3* • *Bredgade 63–5* • *33 11 45 15* • *Open noon–2pm & 6–10pm Mon–Thu, noon–2pm & 6–11pm Fri, 6–11pm Sat, 6–10pm Sun* • *www.lesommelier.dk* • ⓚⓚⓚⓚ

Formel B

9 Beautifully prepared, French-style cuisine using fresh Danish ingredients is the key to the tasty dishes served in this charming restaurant. Winter fare includes raw marinated shrimps with squid and soy-ginger browned butter *(see p87)*.

Meet the Danes

10 If you fancy some good, traditional Danish home cooking and want to see how the locals live, Meet the Danes is an organization that gives you the opportunity to do just that. Guests are allocated a Danish host who will cook them dinner in their own home. Booking ahead is advised. ○ *23 28 43 47* • *www.meetthedanes.dk*

Top 10 Danish Dishes

Frikadeller
1 Pork and veal meatballs, fried in butter and usually served with potatoes.

Stegt Flæsk
2 A classic Danish dish. Fried slices of pork on the bone with a creamy parsley sauce and potatoes.

Smørrebrødsmad
3 An open sandwich usually made with rye bread. Beef with horseradish sauce is a popular topping.

Skipperlabskovs
4 Beef, marinated for 24 hours in brine and stewed with potatoes, bay leaves and black peppercorns.

Sol Over Gudhjem
5 A typical Bornholm dish. Smoked herring, topped with egg yolk, onion and chives.

Marinerede Sild
6 Herring, marinated in vinegar and spices, served with onion and capers. Tastes best with rye bread.

Rødkål
7 A common way of cooking Rødkål (red cabbage) is stewing it for 40 minutes with apples, vinegar and sugar.

Kogt Hamburgerryg
8 A Danish staple of pork loin cooked with thyme and parsley, accompanied by boiled potatoes and vegetables; horseradish or mustard sauce is often added for taste.

Ris à l'Amande
9 Rice pudding with almonds, served cold and topped with warm cherry sauce. A popular Christmas-time dessert.

Gulerodskage
10 Carrot cake made with walnuts and often served with whipped cream.

Left **Thé à la Menthe** Right **Emmerys Bakery**

Cafés and Bars

Laundromat Café

Bastionen + Løven
Set inside an old mill in Christianshavn, this is one of the most romantic eateries in Copenhagen. It is famous for its weekend brunches, so try to get there early *(see p93)*.

Laundromat Café
There is a lot you can do at this cheerful "hybrid" café. You can pop your laundry into one of the Laundromat machines and relax with a cup of coffee, or have lunch. You can also browse through the newspapers and hundreds of books on display. ✎ *Map C3 • Elmegade 15, Nørrebro • 35 35 26 72 • www.thelaundromatcafe.com • ⓚⓚ*

Emmerys Bakery
One of several branches, this is Denmark's foremost organic gourmet store. Primarily a bakery, it also sells sandwiches, drinks and beautifully packaged gourmet food. It has a nice café where you can sample their goods any time from breakfast onwards. ✎ *Map L4 • St Strandstræde 21*

Rabes Have
This 17th-century pub is the oldest in Copenhagen. It has a tasteful decor, with dark green and white walls and a pretty garden at the back. The food served here is mostly organic, and traditional open sandwiches are offered at lunchtime *(see p93)*.

Pussy Galore's Flying Circus
This was one of the first cafés to open in trendy Nørrebro. They serve good food and in the summer, you can sit out on the cobbled square and enjoy your snack *(see p79)*.

Kontiki Bar & Færgen Ellen
This refreshing bar is set on a boat, just behind the Opera House on Holmen. Located far from the bustle of busy tourist areas, you can sit out on the deck for drinks and snacks, or have a more formal meal in the cabin. It is advisable to book ahead. ✎ *Map M4 • Takkelloftvej 1Z • Open May–Sep only • 40 50 90 48 • www.kontikibar.dk • ⓚⓚⓚ*

Cafe Retro
This non-profit café just off Strøget is run by an international group of volunteers. It offers soup, tapas, cake and hot and cold drinks at low prices. Spread over two floors, the decor consists of comfort-

Discover more at www.dk.com

Pussy Galore's Flying Circus

able sofas and candle-lit coffee tables. ⌖ *Map J4 • Knabrostræde 26 • Open noon–11pm Tue–Thu and Sun, noon–1am Fri–Sat • www.cafe-retro. dk •* ⓦ

Thé à la Menthe

This lovely little basement Moroccan tea salon offers great cold drinks, tea and meze, as well as serving warm Moroccan dishes, salads and samosas. The decor is Moroccan, with kilims and water pipes. Yet, it retains a Danish feel with cream-coloured wall panelling and pale green divans. ⌖ *Map J5 • Rådhusstræde 5b • 33 33 00 38 •* ⓦ

Salonen

This wonderfully cosy café is a firm favourite with both international students and locals. The laid-back atmosphere makes Salonen a great place to lounge and relax – and even have your hair cut – with a large cup of coffee or tea. For those in need of greater sustenance, the friendly staff serve up hearty food from the fusion/crossover menu – prepared in a tiny kitchen. There are DJs at the weekend. ⌖ *Map H4 • Sankt Peders Stræde 20 • 50 19 18 11 • Open 11am–midnight Mon–Wed, 11am–1am Thu–Sat, 11am–11pm Sun •* ⓦ

La Glace

Located just off Strøget, La Glace is one of the foremost (and the oldest) confectioneries in Copenhagen, offering mouth-watering cakes and chocolates. Both coffee and cakes are beautifully presented, and they are best savoured in the Old-World ambience created by the traditional polished-wood interiors. ⌖ *Map H4 • Skoubogade 3–5 • 33 14 46 46 • Open 8:30am–6pm Mon–Fri, 9am–6pm Sat (also 10am–6pm Sun Oct–Easter) • www.laglace.dk •* ⓦ

The interior of La Glace

 For more cafés and bars, see pp52–5, 79, 81 and 93.

A night out at Culture Box

Nightlife Venues

Søpavillonen

Søpavillonen
Great tribute bands perform at this stunning lakeside pavilion, which has been transformed into a restaurant, bar and spacious dance floor. DJs play a mix of 1970s and 1980s disco, with elements of Latin, rock and Danish pop.
◈ Map C4 • Gyldenløvesgade 24 • 33 15 12 24 • Nightclub: 11pm–5am Fri–Sat • Over 18s only • www.soepavillonen.dk

Rust
Trendy Rust is at the cutting edge of the local music and clubbing scene. It showcases up-and-coming acts, live music sets and top international DJs. They combine to provide an eclectic mix of sounds both in the bar and the basement club (see p81).

Park Diskotek
This sophisticated venue plays an exciting range of music including house and R&B. There are several dance floors here which provide an authentic 1970s atmosphere (see p81).

Karriere Bar
This cocktail bar and restaurant in the meat-packing district is owned by artist Jeppe Hein and his sister Lærke. The entire bar is an installation piece, lit by lamps made by artist Olafur Eliasson (see p35). ◈ Map C6 • Flæsketorvet 57–67 • 33 21 55 09 • Open 8pm–midnight Thu, 8pm–4am Fri–Sat • www.karrierebar.com

Hive
The city's old courthouse has been transformed into a modern nightclub complete with iPhone chargers at the tables. Some of Copenhagen's more exclusive club nights are held here. ◈ Map H4 • Skindergade 45–7 • 28 45 74 67 • Open 11pm–6am Fri–Sat • www.hive.dk

Gefährlich
Located in the heart of Nørrebro, known for its club culture, Gefährlich (German for "dangerous") has a restaurant, bar, art gallery, coffee shop, boutique and record store. Its nightclub caters to the tastes of the young and hip (see p81).

Rust

For more nightlife venues, see pp70 and 81.

Club Mambo

Ideal Bar
7 On the ground floor of trendy venue VEGA *(see also p43)*, this lounge bar offers club nights with a local vibe. It is an inexpensive midweek option. 🔊 Map B6 • Enghavevej 40 • 33 25 70 11 • Open 8pm–1am selected Weds, 9pm–2am Thu, 10pm–5am Fri–Sat • www.idealbar.vega.dk

Culture Box
8 This purist techno club is one of Copenhagen's leading venues for electronic music. Its cocktail bar opens earlier than the club and makes a good meeting place. 🔊 Map K2 • Kronprinsessegade 54 • 33 32 50 50 • Open 11pm–6am Fri–Sat (Cocktail Box open from 9pm) • Closed Jun–Jul • Min age 18 • www.culture-box.com

Nord Natklub
9 A popular nightclub catering exclusively for the over-30s and located in the brightly coloured Palads building. Free entry for Tivoli ticket holders on Fridays, for post-concert parties. 🔊 Map G5 • Axeltorv 5 • Open 10pm–4am Fri, 10pm–5am Sat • Min age 30 • Adm • www.nordnatklub.dk

Club Mambo
10 This is the place to "feel the Latin spirit". An energetic and colourful club, it is one of the hottest salsa clubs in the city. Take advantage of free salsa and merengue classes *(see p70)*.

Top 10 Microbreweries

Mikkeller
1 Set up in 2006, this has its own pub. 🔊 Viktoriagade 8, Vesterbro • 33 31 04 15 • www.mikkeller.dk

Nørrebro Bryghus
2 Take a tour of the brewery; taste some beer. 🔊 Ryesgade 3, Nørrebro • 35 30 05 30 • www.noerrebrobryghus.dk

Vesterbro Bryghus
3 Six beers brewed to traditional Austrian recipes. 🔊 Vesterbrogade 2B • 33 11 17 05 • www.vesterbrobryghus.dk

Færgekroen
4 Two hand-brewed beers on offer. 🔊 Tivoli • 33 75 06 80 • www.faergekroen.dk

Brewpub
5 Beer garden in a 17th-century building. 🔊 Vestergade 29 • 33 32 00 60 • Closed Sun • www.brewpub.dk

Bryggeriet Apollo
6 One of the original local microbreweries. 🔊 Vesterbrogade 3 • 33 12 33 13 • www.bryggeriet.dk

Herslev Bryghus
7 This small brewery has a shop in its yard and gives tours by appointment. 🔊 Kattingevej 8, Herslev, Roskilde • 46 40 18 07

Bryggeri Skovlyst
8 Located in the Hareskoven woods, this microbrewery also has a restaurant. 🔊 Skovlystvej 2, Værløse • 44 98 65 45

Amager Bryghus
9 Tours Mon–Sat by appointment. 🔊 Fuglebækvej 2C • 32 50 62 00 • www.amagerbryghus.dk

Copenhagen Beer Festival
10 Beer festival held each May in an old Carlsberg tapping plant. 🔊 Tap 1, Ny Carlsbergvej 91, Vesterbro • www.beerfestival.dk

Left **Centralhjørnet** Right **Masken Bar & Café**

🔟 Gay and Lesbian Venues

1 Centralhjørnet
This is Copenhagen's oldest gay bar, dating from 1852. It holds drag nights; regular shows take place on Thursdays. Kylie Minogue and Europop are jukebox favourites. Sunday afternoons are usually packed.
🟦 *Map H4* • *Kattesundet 18* • *33 11 85 49* • *Open noon–2am Sun–Thu, noon–3am Fri–Sat* • *www.centralhjornet.dk*

2 Vela
Attracting a mixed crowd, Vela is a popular lesbian bar with oriental decor in the Vesterbro area. There's table football, small booths and a selection of cheap beers. 🟦 *Map C4* • *Viktoriagade 2–4* • *33 14 34 19* • *Open 9pm–midnight Wed, 9pm–4am Thu, 9pm–5am Fri–Sat* • *www.velagayclub.dk*

3 Jailhouse
Kitted out as a prison, this café and event bar has booths like prison cells and staff dressed as prison guards or police officers. There is a restaurant on the second floor; the atmosphere here is more sedate. 🟦 *Map H4* • *Studiestræde 12* • *33 15 22 55* • *Open 3pm–2am Sun–Thu, 3pm–5am Fri–Sat; Restaurant: 6–9pm Wed–Fri* • *www.jailhousecph.dk*

4 Oscar Bar and Café
A bar and café for the style-conscious, with a long bar and posh leather furniture. The DJ plays funky disco and soulful deep house on weekends. 🟦 *Map H5* • *Rådhuspladsen 77* • *33 12 09 99* • *Open 11am–11pm Sun–Thu, 11am–2am Fri & Sat (kitchen till 4pm daily)* • *www. oscarbarcafe.dk*

5 Café Intime
Founded in 1913, this kitsch bar has a predominantly gay crowd. A pianist plays popular classics (don't be afraid to sing along); you can also enjoy jazz on Sundays. 🟦 *Map B5* • *Allégade 25, 2000 Frederiksberg* • *38 34 19 58* • *Open 6pm–2am daily* • *www.cafeintime.dk*

6 Amigo Bar
This popular bar pulsates with a lively party atmosphere well into the early hours. Its speciality is camp karaoke.
🟦 *Map C5* • *Schønbergsgade 4 (corner of Gammel Kongevej), 2000 Frederiksberg* • *33 21 49 15* • *Open 10pm–7am daily*

7 Club Christopher
Named after New York's Christopher Street, this club caters for a range of crowds with

Jailhouse

Oscar Bar and Café

an easy-going, hard-partying atmosphere. There are several dance floors, with both in-house and guest DJs. The door charge includes a free bar. ✆ *Map J4 • Knabostræde 3 • 60 80 71 76 • Open midnight–5am Fri, 11pm–5am Sat • Min age 18*

Mens Bar
This strictly all-male, no-frills bar is filled with leather, fascinating tattoos and a dash of denim. Try to catch the free Danish brunch at 3pm on the first Sunday of the month. ✆ *Map H4 • Teglgårdsstræde 3 • 33 12 73 03 • Open 3pm–2am daily • www. mensbar.dk*

Masken Bar & Café
The younger crowd at this venue starts buzzing after midnight. It has exciting live music and drag shows, spread across two floors. ✆ *Map H4 • Studiestræde 33 • 33 91 09 37 • Open 2pm–3am Sun–Thu, 2pm–5am Fri–Sat • www.maskenbar.dk*

Meet Gay Copenhagen
You can meet and dine with local gays and lesbians in the comfort of their homes. Hosts are very friendly and usually offer traditional fare. It's best to book a dinner well in advance. Note: this is not a dating agency. ✆ *27 21 80 65 • www.meetgaycopenhagen.dk*

Top 10 Gay & Lesbian Festivals & Events

1 Mix Copenhagen Film Festival
Ten-day lesbian, gay, bi and trans film festival held annually in October at venues city-wide. ✆ • www.mixcopenhagen.dk

2 Copenhagen Pride Festival
Week-long festival in August. Includes the gay pride parade. ✆ www.copenhagenpride.dk

3 Mr Gay
Pan Club's popular, good-humoured beauty pageant for gays. ✆ www.mrgay.dk

4 Rainbow Festival
Ten days of art exhibitions, drag shows, dancing and parades just across the bridge in Malmö, Sweden. ✆ www.rfsl.se/malmo

5 World Aids Day
Commemorated each year on 1 Dec.

6 Pan Idræt
Gay and lesbian sports club for a variety of activities, including swimming, badminton and rugby. ✆ www.panidraet.dk

7 Nordic Open
Dance competition for same-sex couples on 30 December every year. ✆ www.pandans.dk/nordicopen.htm

8 Torchlight Procession
This event in memory of people who have died of AIDS takes place on the last Sunday in May. ✆ www.aidsfondet.dk

9 St Hans
Annual bonfire and beach party on Amager Beach on Sankt Hans Night, 23 June. ✆ www.copenhagen-gay-life.dk

10 Queer Festival
Musicians, activists and drag kings and queens; late July. ✆ www.queerfestival.org

Left **Children's Museum at the Nationalmuseet** Right **Classic car rides, Tivoli**

🔟 Places for Children

Guinness World Records Museum

1 Guinness World Records Museum

This highly popular attraction brings the Guinness World Records to life. From the bizarre, such as bicycle-eating men, to the internationally renowned in sport and science, 13 galleries celebrate strangeness, ingenuity and determination *(see p66)*.

2 Statens Museum for Kunst

The Children's Art Museum at the National Gallery caters for children aged between 4 and 12, with work-shops where kids can draw, paint and sculpt and a sketching room. There is a family day on the first Sunday of each month with guided museum tours *(see pp22–3)*.

3 Wonderful World of H C Andersen Museum

Explore the life of Hans Christian Andersen, Denmark's national hero, at this charming museum. It is aimed at kids who will enjoy the tableaux and recordings of some of his fairy tales (in several languages). The hand-written manuscript of *The Stone and the Wise Man* (1858) may interest bibliophiles *(see p66)*.

4 Nationalmuseet

The National Museum includes an interesting Children's Museum. Rather than just looking at things, children are encouraged to participate in numerous activities, like dressing up in grandma's clothes to see how different they are from today's garments, or sitting in an old Danish classroom, learning about medieval castles *(see pp26–7)*.

5 Tøjhusmuseet

The Royal Arsenal Museum, on the island of Slotsholmen, is a popular tourist site and is home to Christian IV's original arsenal (1604–8). The ground floor, in particular, evokes the atmosphere of those days, with a long arched cavern and canons along walls *(see pp28–9)*.

Hands-on fun for kids at Experimentarium

Experimentarium

This innovative science centre brings science to life through hands-on exploration. Most exhibits are interactive, allowing kids to perform over 300 experiments. Environmental issues are high on the agenda and adults will have as much fun as the kids. ⊗ *Map L6 (until 2016)* • *Trangravsvej 12, Christianshavn* • *39 27 33 33* • *Open Jul–mid-Aug: 10am–8pm daily; mid-Aug–Jun: 10am–5pm Mon–Fri (to 6pm Sat & Sun)* • *Adm charge; free for 0–2 year olds* • *Dis access* • *www.experimentarium.dk*

Den Blå Planet

The national aquarium is the largest in Northern Europe, with over 20,000 marine life forms and 7 million litres of water. The aquarium's architecture is worthy of as much attention as its exhibits *(see p99)*.

Dried seahorse, Den Blå Planet

Zoologisk Have

This zoo is Denmark's largest cultural institution, attracting around 1.2 million visitors every year. Besides the tigers, polar bears and elephants, there are thematic adventure trails and a children's petting zoo. In spring, there tend to be many new baby animals *(see p83)*.

Tivoli

The best time to take kids to Tivoli is during the day, when the atmosphere is more family-oriented. The many fun rides include cars on tracks, dragon boats on the lake, the pantomime theatre and the trolley bus. There are changing facilities, and plenty of child-friendly places to eat *(see pp10–13)*.

Ripley's Believe It or Not!

While adults may find the collection of bizarre, freakish curiosities on display a little unsettling, kids love it! The Ecuadorian shrunken heads are a particularly gruesome highlight. ⊗ *Map H5* • *Rådhuspladsen 57* • *33 32 31 31* • *Open mid-Jun–Aug: 10am–10pm daily; Sep–mid-Jun: 10am–6pm daily (to 8pm Fri–Sat)* • *Adm*

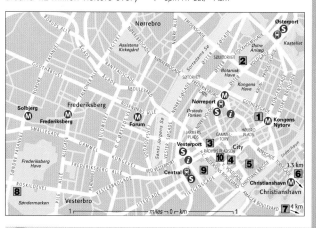

Left **Christian VIII's Palace, Amalienborg** Right **Vor Frue Kirke, detail of façade**

Top 10 Sights of Royal Copenhagen

1 Amalienborg
This royal residence consists of four palaces arranged around a square. Two of the palaces function as museums and are open to the public, while the other two are royal homes and remain closed. Queen Margrethe resides in Christian IX's Palace and Crown Prince Frederik in Frederik VIII's Palace. An interesting museum housed in Christian VIII's Palace includes reconstructed rooms from the 19th century *(see pp20–21)*.

2 Rosenborg Slot
This delightful, turreted Renaissance palace, built by Christian IV, is the oldest royal palace standing in its original form. It is also a depository for the crown jewels *(see pp14–15)*.

3 Royal Copenhagen Porcelain
This was one of the first porcelain factories outside Germany.

Christiansborg Slot

The traditional Royal Copenhagen design, "Blue Floral", dates back to the factory's initiation in 1775. The pottery features a blue design because in earlier times, cobalt was the only colour that was able to withstand high firing temperatures *(see p68)*.

4 Vor Frue Kirke
St Mary's Cathedral has been a place of royal worship and ceremony since the 13th century and was the setting for the marriage of Margrethe I to Håkon VI of Norway in 1363. Since then, Christian I (1449) and Crown Prince Frederik (2004) have been married here and several princes have been crowned *(see pp16–17)*.

5 Christiansborg Slot
This is the seventh castle to have been built upon this site. The first, Bishop Absalon's fortified castle (1167), was destroyed in 1369. The castle built in 1730 was the first to be called Christiansborg; it was destroyed by fire in 1794. The present castle is home to the Danish Parliament *(see pp28–9)*.

6 Crown Jewels
These symbols of monarchy, kept in the stronghold basement of Rosenborg Slot, include the crown, sceptre, orb, sword of state, ampulla (flask for anointing the monarch) and royal jewellery.

7 Fredensborg Slot
This 18th-century Baroque palace is the Queen's summer

Rosenborg Slot

home. The beautiful gardens are among Denmark's largest. ✆ *33 40 31 87 • Open only in Jul 1–4:30pm daily (with guided tours); Reserved gardens: Jul 9am–5pm • Adm; free entry to gardens • Bus 173E, direction Fredensborg*

Frederiksborg Slot
Christian IV built this Dutch Renaissance-style castle between 1600 and 1620. It is notable for its spires, copper roofs and sweeping gables. After it was destroyed in a fire in 1859, the Carlsberg Brewery magnate Jacob Jacobsen helped rebuild it. The gardens, dating from 1720–25, are the only royal gardens to have escaped being updated to the 19th-century Romantic style *(see pp98–9)*.

Roskilde Domkirke
Danish royals, including Harald Bluetooth *(see p33)*, have been buried at Roskilde since the 12th century. The cathedral now houses 39 tombs, the oldest belonging to Margrethe I (d.1412) *(see p100)*.

Kronborg Slot
This castle, built as a fortress in the 15th century, was used as a prison and army barracks until 1922. It is now occasionally used for royal functions. You may even hear a salute being fired whenever the royal yacht passes by *(see p102)*.

Crown Jewels

Christian IV's Crown
Made in 1595–6 by Dirich Fyring, with diamond, gold, enamel and pearls.

The Queen's Crown
Made for Queen Sophie Magdalene in 1731. The large, square table-cut diamonds are believed to have come from Queen Sophie Amalie's crown (1648).

Christian V's Crown
Christian V's Absolutist crown (1670–71). Its large, rare sapphire is believed to be a present from the Duke of Milan to Christian I in 1474.

Regalia
Sceptre, orb, globe and ampulla made for Frederik III's coronation. Used at subsequent coronations until 1840.

Order of the Elephant
Founded by Christian I around 1450. The chain is made of gold, enamel, diamonds and pearls.

Order of the Dannebrog
Established in 1671 as part of the measures introduced by the Absolute monarchs to manage their subjects.

Jewellery Sets
Includes pearl set (1840), made from Charlotte Amalie's jewellery; diamond set (18th century); emerald set (1723).

Oldenburg Horn
Enamelled, silver-gilt drinking horn (around 1465).

The King's Law 1665
Absolutism's constitution, made from parchment, silk, gold and silver.

Baptismal Set
Four-piece, gold and silver baptismal set (1671), thought to have been first used for Crown Prince Frederik.

AROUND TOWN

Tivoli North to
Gothersgade
62–71

Nørrebro, Østerbro
and North
of Gothersgade
74–81

Vesterbro and
Frederiksberg
82–87

Christianshavn
and Holmen
88–93

Beyond
Copenhagen
96–103

COPENHAGEN'S TOP 10

Left **Ny Carlsberg Glyptotek** Right **Kongens Nytorv**

Tivoli North to Gothersgade

RICH IN HISTORY, *this area is a popular entertainment destination. Heading northeast of Tivoli, which was originally outside the city walls, you can walk back in time through the old town that evolved during the Middle Ages – though much of it succumbed to fire in the 18th century – to Slotsholmen, the site where the first dwellings that became Copenhagen were built in the 12th century. Along the way, you will find great shopping areas, museums, an old town and a royal palace.*

Sights

1 Tivoli
2 Rådhuset
3 Astronomical Clock
4 Ny Carlsberg Glyptotek
5 Nationalmuseet
6 Kunstforeningen Gammel Strand
7 Amagertov
8 Latin Quarter
9 Kongens Nytorv and Nyhavn
10 Slotsholmen

Amagertorv

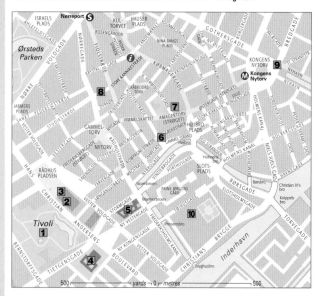

Preceding pages: **Marmorkirken and Amalienborg, seen from Amaliehaven.**

The Nimb building in Tivoli

Tivoli

Tivoli has virtually become synonymous with Copenhagen and should be high on the list for any visitor. In season, this park buzzes with the sounds of exhilarating rides. It is not only for adventure-seekers though. At night, the setting turns magical and romantic, with fairy lights and Japanese lanterns glowing in the darkness and music in the air *(see pp10–11)*.

Rådhuset

The Copenhagen Rådhus, or town hall, is a mock-Gothic building replete with fantastical sea creatures, built in 1892–1905 and designed by architect Martin Nyrop. Its 105.6-m (346-ft) tower affords superb views of the city. Take a tour, or just pop in to see the pre-Raphaelitesque entrance way, or the Italianate reception hall. Many Copenhageners get married here, so you may just see several wedding parties on the steps. ◈ *Map H5 • Rådhuspladsen 1 • 33 66 25 86 • Open 9am–4pm Mon–Fri, 9:30am–1pm Sat • Tours in English at 1pm Mon–Fri, 10am Sat; Tower tour 11am & 2pm Mon–Fri, noon Sat • Adm for tours and tower*

Astronomical Clock

This ingenious clock, cased in a mahogany cabinet, was designed by locksmith and watchmaker Jens Olsen. After waiting for 50 years to obtain funds, Olsen started working on the clock in 1943. He died two years later, but work continued and the clock was set in motion in 1955. Famous for its accuracy, this 14,000-part clock loses less than a second a century. It shows local time, solar time, sunrise and sunset times, sidereal time, celestial pole movement and the movement of the planets. ◈ *Map H5 • Rådhus, Rådhuspladsen 1 • 33 66 25 86 • Open 8:30am–4pm Mon–Fri, 10am–1pm Sat • Adm with Rådhus tour*

Ny Carlsberg Glyptotek

This superb art gallery is home to a fascinating collection of Mediterranean, classical and Egyptian art and artifacts. Danish and 19th-century French works of art are also on display, including French Impressionist paintings. The museum is housed in a 19th-century building with a splendid cupola, beneath which lies an indoor winter garden, sculptures and water features. The modern wing is a wonderful, light-filled area *(see pp24–5)*.

Rådhuset

Nationalmuseet

The National Museum is housed inside a former royal residence, dating from the 18th century. The exhibits trace Danish history, from ancient times to the present, including some amazing ethnographic collections. The most popular exhibits chart the history of Danes from the Ice Age to the Viking campaigns (see pp26–7).

Kunstforeningen Gammel Strand

The Gammel Strand art association was formed in 1825 and has been housed in a Philip de Lange-designed building since 1952. The centre puts on five to six changing exhibitions annually, from group shows to retrospectives, both classic and contemporary. There is also an excellent bookshop on the first floor and a pleasant café. Disabled access is through the courtyard at Læderstræde 15. ◎ Map J4
• Gammel Strand 48 • 33 36 02 60
• Open 11am–5pm Tue–Sun (to 8pm Wed)
• Adm; free with Copenhagen
Card • Dis access • www.glstrand.dk

Vor Frue Kirke in the Latin Quarter

Amagertorv

This busy square is situated in the very middle of Strøget (see p66). Note the attractive tiles that were designed by Bjørn Nørgaard. The square's focal point, the Storkespringvandet fountain, provided the inspiration for a Danish folk song of the 1960s, and today is a popular meeting place. The cafés Norden and Europa, situated on either side of the square, are extremely popular. ◎ Map J4

Latin Quarter

To the west of Strøget lies the Latin Quarter, the original home of the University of Copenhagen. It dates back to the Middle Ages when the primary language of culture and education was Latin. Some of the old university buildings are still in use, although much of the campus is now on the island of Amager. If you take a left off Strøget onto Nørregade, you will find the Universitetet and Vor Frue Kirke. Both have been used for their current purposes since the 15th and 13th centuries respectively; the current buildings, however, date back to the 19th century. The Rundetårn on Købmagergade is also worth a visit (see pp16–17).

Kongens Nytorv and Nyhavn

At the top of Nyhavn stands the King's New Square (Kongens Nytorv), an elegant area surrounded by fashionable 18th-century mansions that now house banks, up-market department stores and hotels. It is flanked by the Charlottenborg Slot (now an exhibition space and home to the academy of art) and the Royal Theatre (Det Kongelige Teater).

Teatermuseet in Slotsholmen

Nyhavn (which means "new harbour") is a lively tourist area filled with restaurants, cafés and old sailing boats along the canal quayside. The atmosphere here is a stark contrast to what it was in the 1670s, when sailors, traders and low-lifes frequented the area. When Hans Christian Anderson lived here it was a notorious red-light district. Even until the 1970s, this was not a part of town that many would have visited at night. Urban regeneration has changed all that and on sunny evenings, in particular, you may not find a place to sit down (see pp18–19).

Slotsholmen
A visit to Slotsholmen could take up almost an entire day, as there is plenty to see. Primarily the site of Christiansborg Slot, which burnt down in 1794, it is now home to Denmark's Parliament, and used by the Queen for State functions (you can visit the Royal Reception Rooms on a guided tour). You will find several museums here as well, such as the Tøjhusmuseum, which is filled with historic arms and armour. The delightful Theatre Museum (Teatermuseet) (see p35) is also worth a visit with the main attraction being the 18th-century palace theatre. Other sites include the palace church and the 12th-century ruins of the first Copenhagen castle where its founder, Bishop Absalon, resided (see pp28–9).

Walking Tour

Morning

Start your day at the **Ny Carlsberg Glyptotek** (see p63); don't miss the impressive Egyptian and Impressionist collections. Have an early lunch at the charming **Winter Garden Café** (see pp24–5).

Afternoon

After lunch, cross H C Andersen Boulevard and head to the **Nationalmuseet** to take one of the hour-long tours. Then, stroll to the end of Ny Vestergade until you reach Frederiks Kanal. Cross the bridge and visit **Christiansborg Slot** (see p28). If you arrive by 2pm, pop into the stables, the **Teatermuseet** (see p35) and the ruins before taking a tour of the State Rooms at 3pm. Then, walk back over the bridge and turn right onto Gammel Strand (note the **Fishwife statue**, see p37) for afternoon snacks at one of the restaurants and cafés. Walk down Købmagergade via Højbro Plads, right up to **Rundetårn** (see p16). If you are feeling energetic, hike to the top for a good view of the city. Heading back down, take a left from Strøget and keep walking until you reach **Kongens Nytorv and Nyhavn** – a perfect spot for a relaxing evening drink and supper at one of the quayside bars and restaurants. Instead of heading back via Strøget, take the less mainstream Lille Strandstræde. Walk to Rådhuspladsen and go across to **Tivoli** (see pp10–11). Spend the evening at these lovely gardens enjoying the atmosphere.

Left **Statue of H C Andersen** Centre **Caritas Springvandet** Right **A shop on Strøget**

Best of the Rest

1 Domhus
The courthouse was built in 1805–15. The "Bridge of Sighs" across Slutterigade (prison street) was crossed by prisoners being led to trial. ◈ *Map H4 • Nytorv 25 • Open 8:30am–4pm Mon–Thu (to 3pm Fri)*

2 Rådhuspladsen
On the southwestern end of Strøget, the town hall square is one of the liveliest areas of the city. ◈ *Map H5*

3 Statue of H C Andersen
This statue of the author by Henry Lukow-Nielsen dates from 1961. ◈ *Map H5*

4 Caritas Springvandet
Dating back to 1608, the Charity Fountain is one of the oldest in the city. ◈ *Map H4*

5 Guinness World Records Museum
As the name suggests, this museum shows 500 Guinness records. ◈ *Map K4 • Østergade 16 • 33 32 31 31 • Open Sep–mid-Jun: 10am–6pm daily (to 8pm Fri–Sat); mid-Jun–Aug: 10am–10pm daily • Adm (combined ticket with H C Andersen Museum available)*

6 Wonderful World of HC Andersen Museum
Scenes from Andersen's fairy tales and other memorabilia are found here. ◈ *Map H5 • 33 32 31 31 • Open Sep–mid-Jun: 10am–6pm daily (to 8pm Fri–Sat); mid-Jun–Aug: 10am–10pm daily • Adm; free with Copenhagen Card*

7 Post & Telemuseet
Located next to the main post office, this museum charts the history of communication from the 17th century onwards. ◈ *Map J4 • Købmagergade 37 • 33 41 09 00 • Open 10am–4pm daily • www.ptt-museum.dk*

8 Gammel Strand
This canalside street is home to excellent restaurants, one of the city's best flea markets and an admirable art museum (Kunstforeningen Gammel Strand, see p64). It is also a pick-up point for Stromma Canal Tours (see p8). ◈ *Map J4*

9 Georg Jensen Museum
The jewellery and homeware of the famous silversmith are on display here. ◈ *Map J4 • Amagertorv 4 • 33 14 02 29 • Open 10am–6pm Mon–Thu, 10am–7pm Fri, 10am–5pm Sat (Jun–Sep Sun) • www.georgjensen.com*

10 Strøget
This is the name given to the five main, interconnected shopping streets of Copenhagen. ◈ *Map H5–K4*

Price Categories

For a three-course meal for one without alcohol, including taxes and extra charges.

⊛	up to 200 Dkr
⊛⊛	200–300
⊛⊛⊛	300–400
⊛⊛⊛⊛	400–500
⊛⊛⊛⊛⊛	over 500 Dkr

Riz Raz Sticks 'n' Veggies

🔟 Dining

1 Riz Raz Sticks 'n' Veggies
Riz Raz is famous for its great value, Mediterranean-influenced vegetarian buffets, as well as meaty kebabs. ◍ *Map J5 • Kompagnistræde 20 • 33 15 05 75 • www.rizraz.dk • ⊛*

2 L'Alsace
This gourmet restaurant specializes in dishes from Alsace, with an emphasis on fresh fish and seafood. ◍ *Map K4 • Ny Østergade 9 • 33 14 57 43 • Closed Sun & public holidays • www.alsace.dk • ⊛⊛⊛*

3 Alberto K
One of the best restaurants in Denmark, Alberto K offers a blend of Scandinavian-Italian flavours. ◍ *Map G5 • Radisson Blu Royal Hotel, 20th Floor, Hammerichsgade 1 • 33 42 61 61 • Closed Sun & public holidays • Book ahead • www.alberto-k.dk • ⊛⊛⊛⊛⊛*

4 Geist
Stylish eatery, both lavish and informal; compose your meal from a long list of small- and medium-sized dishes, including good vegetarian options. ◍ *Map K4 • Kongens Nytorv 8 • 33 13 37 13 • Book ahead • www.restaurantgeist.dk • ⊛⊛⊛*

5 Bror
This small restaurant in the Latin Quarter offers innovative seasonal Scandinavian dishes from two former Noma chefs *(see p49)*. ◍ *Map H4 • Skt. Peders Stræde 24A • 32 17 59 99 • Open 5:30pm–midnight Wed–Sun • www.restaurantbror.dk • ⊛⊛⊛*

6 Krogs Fiskerestaurant
This landmark fish restaurant offers organic and sustainable lunch menus. ◍ *Map J4 • Gammel Strand 38 • 33 15 89 15 • Open daily (Sun lunch only) • www.krogs.dk • ⊛⊛⊛⊛*

7 Atlas Bar
Exotic dishes served in a cool basement location. ◍ *Map H4 • Larsbjørnsstræde 18 • 33 15 03 52 • Closed Sun • www.atlasbar.dk • ⊛*

8 Bankeråt
Enjoy steaks, salads and a selection of beers in this artistic venue. ◍ *Map G3 • Ahlefeldtsgade 29 • 33 93 69 88 • www.bankeraat.dk • ⊛*

9 Restaurant Peder Oxe
A well-established restaurant on a picturesque square. ◍ *Map J4 • Gråbrødretov 11 • 33 11 00 77 • Open 11:30am–11pm daily • www.pederoxe.dk • ⊛⊛⊛*

10 Husmanns Vinstue
This wine cellar/pub/restaurant offers traditional herring-based dishes. ◍ *Map H4 • Larsbjørnsstræde 2 • 33 11 58 86 • Open for lunch only, Mon–Sat • www.husmannsvinstue.dk • ⊛⊛*

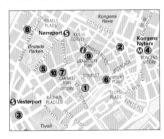

Left **Birger Christensen** Centre **Illum Department Store** Right **Royal Copenhagen shop**

Strøget Shopping

Illums Bolighus
This shrine to stylish interior design and kitchenware (mainly Italian and Danish) offers everything from Royal Copenhagen porcelain to groovy dog-biscuit dispensers and objects d'art. ⊗ *Map J4 • Amagertorv 10 • 33 14 19 41 • Open Sun • www.illumsbolighus.dk*

Royal Copenhagen Porcelain
This flagship store offers a range of designs, from the classic 18th-century *flora danica* design to the modern and organic. ⊗ *Map J4 • Amagertorv 6 • 33 13 71 81 • Open Sun • www.royalcopenhagen.com*

Illum Department Store
This stylish, six-storied department store offers quality clothing and homeware. There are also several cafés, a bakery and a supermarket. ⊗ *Map K4 • Østergade 52 • 33 14 40 02 • www.illum.eu*

Birger Christensen
This exclusive fashion store sells Birger Christensen coats and jackets, as well as a wide collection of international labels. ⊗ *Map K4 • Østergade 38 • 33 11 55 55 • www.birger-christensen.com*

Georg Jensen
Georg Jensen's superb designs are available at the historic firm's flagship store, including stylish jewellery, watches, cutlery, candlesticks, antiques and even designer sunglasses. ⊗ *Map J4 • Amagertorv 4 • 33 11 40 80 • www.georgjensen.com*

Mads Nørgaard
Sells classic, casual Danish menswear, including the timeless trademark, unisex, striped top. ⊗ *Map J4 • Amagertov 15 • 33 32 01 28 • www.madsnorgaard.com*

Noa Noa
Offers women's cottons, linens and silks in pretty styles with a similar collection for girls aged 3–12. ⊗ *Map K4 • Østergade 6 • 29 74 31 66 • www.noa-noa.dk*

Hay House
In addition to the store on Pilestræde, a larger branch has opened above Café Norden on Amagertov. Filled with bright plastic furniture and accessories. ⊗ *Map J4 • Østergade 61, 2nd Floor • 42 82 08 20 • www.hay.dk*

A Pair
Here you will find fashionable footwear for men and women, as well as leather bags and belts with large, silver buckles. It is a chain with shops all over Denmark. ⊗ *Map K4 • Ny Østergade 3 • 33 91 99 20 • www.apair.dk*

Sand
This Danish fashion house offers a range of stylish and classic clothing and accessories for men and women. ⊗ *Map K4 • Østergade 40 • 33 14 21 21 • www.sand-europe.com*

Strøget has no street sign: it's local speak for Frederiksberggade, Nygade, Vimmelskaftet, Amagertorv and Østergade combined.

Left **Sneaky Fox boutique** Right **Magasin du Nord**

TOP 10 Shops off Strøget

Munthe
The award-winning design duo Munthe plus Simonsen have parted company. Munthe continues to offer wearable women's clothing and accessories with a stylish edge. ◉ Map K4 • Grønnegade 10 • 33 32 03 12 • www.munthe.com

Liebe
A wide range of fun ceramics in pretty pastel shades, all original designs by the owner, Susan Liebe. There are gift ideas in the basement. ◉ Map J5 • Kompagnistræde 23 • 33 93 18 46 • www.liebeshop.dk

Magasin du Nord
This is one of the city's oldest department stores, offering an up-market selection of clothing and homeware. There is also a supermarket and places to eat. The discount sales in January and late summer are very good. ◉ Map K4 • Kongens Nytorv 13 • 33 11 44 33 • Open Sun • www.magasin.dk

Sneaky Fox
This trendy women's boutique is especially well known for its variety of stockings, from the silly to the sophisticated. ◉ Map H4 • Studiestræde 25A • 33 91 25 20 • www.sneakyfox.dk

Marc by Marc Jacobs
Clothing and accessories for both men and women in this spacious and stylish store from the renowned US designer. ◉ Map J3 • Christian IX's Gade 3–5 • 88 19 09 88 • www.marcjacobs.com

Grønlykke
Visit this funky shop if you are looking for colourful and kitsch household accessories, from kitchen bar stools to chandeliers. ◉ Map J4 • Læderstræde 3–5 • 33 13 00 81 • Open first Sun of the month

Henrik Vibskov
The enfant terrible of Danish design has his flagship store in the Latin Quarter. Including his own lines, this shop also stocks other brands given the Vibskov seal of approval. ◉ Map J4 • Krystalgade 6 • 33 14 61 00 • www.henrikvibskovboutique.com

Akimbo
This is a great place for presents, especially for little girls, ranging from edible-looking candle cakes, to jewellery and kitsch toys. ◉ Map J4 • Hyskenstræde 3 • 33 11 13 01

Wettergren & Wettergren
Hidden away down a few steps leading to a basement, this charming shop sells vintage clothing and accessories with a modern twist. ◉ Map J4 • Læderstræde 5 • 33 13 14 05

Stilleben
This tiny shop is filled with beautiful porcelain ceramics, in a range of subtle colours, all created by young Danish potters and ceramic designers. ◉ Map J4 • Niels Hemmingsens Gade 3 • 33 91 11 31 • www.stilleben.dk

Around Town – Tivoli North to Gothersgade

All shops are closed on Sunday unless otherwise specified.

Left **Jazzhouse** Right **Ruby**

Nightlife

Studenterhuset
This charmingly grotty bar serves beer to students at discounted prices, and hosts local bands. ◆ *Map J3 • Købmagergade 52 • www.studenterhuset.com*

Penthouse
The entrance fee for this 1930s-style club includes unlimited soft drinks and draught beer. ◆ *Map H4 • Nørregade 1 • 33 11 74 78 • Open 11pm–6am Fri–Sat • www.penthouse.nu*

Ruby
Exclusive bar styled as an old-fashioned gentlemen's club. ◆ *Map J5 • Nybrogade 10 • 33 93 12 03 • Open 4pm–2am Mon–Sat, 7pm–1am Sun • www.rby.dk*

Grand Teatret
This large, six-screen art-house cinema has a smart, comfortable atmosphere and a small café. ◆ *Map H5 • Mikkel Bryggers Gade 8 • 33 15 16 11 • www.grandteatret.dk*

The Lot
Located in the Galleri K complex next to Strøget, this restaurant becomes a guestlist-only nightclub at weekends. ◆ *Map K4 • Pilestræde 12A • Nightclub open 11pm–3am Fri–Sat • www.thelot.dk*

Bar Rouge
This is one of the hippest cocktail bars in the city, with tastefully designed interiors. ◆ *Map H4 • Hotel Skt Petri, Krystalgade 22 • 33 45 98 22 • www.hotelsktpetri.com*

Jazzhus Montmartre
This legendary jazz venue may now lack an underground feel, but still attracts world class jazz. ◆ *Map K3 • Store Regnegade 19A • 70 26 32 67 • Open 5:30–11:30pm Thu–Sat; concerts start 8pm • Book ahead • Adm • www.jazzhusmontmartre.dk*

Jazzhouse
This live jazz venue attracts both international bands and home-grown talent. ◆ *Map J4 • Niels Hemmingsens Gade 10 • 33 15 47 00 • Open from 7pm for concerts only • www.jazzhouse.dk*

1105
The bartenders at this hip cocktail bar mix some of the best drinks in the city. ◆ *Map K4 • Kristen Bernikows Gade 4 • 33 93 11 05 • Open 8pm–2am Wed, Thu & Sat, 4pm–2am Fri • Closed Sun–Tue • www.1105.dk*

Club Mambo
Dance to salsa in the club, or visit the lounge for reggae and modern hits. ◆ *Map H5 • Vester Voldgade 85 • 33 11 97 66 • Open 9pm–5am Fri–Sat, 8pm–midnight Tue & Thu • www.clubmambo.dk*

Charlie's Bar

Price Categories	
For a three-course meal for one without alcohol, including taxes and extra charges.	⊛ up to 200 Dkr
	⊛⊛ 200–300
	⊛⊛⊛ 300–400
	⊛⊛⊛⊛ 400–500
	⊛⊛⊛⊛⊛ over 500 Dkr

Historic Wining and Dining

1 Vandkunsten Sandwich Bar
This popular sandwich bar is housed in what was Copenhagen's oldest butcher's shop. ⊛ *Map J5* • *Rådhusstræde 17* • *33 13 90 40* • *Closed Sat–Sun* • ⊛

2 Skindbuksen
Founded in 1728, mariners, locals and tourists now rub shoulders at this unpretentious restaurant. ⊛ *Map K4* • *Lille Kongensgade 4* • *33 12 90 37* • *Book ahead* • *www.skindbuksen.dk* • ⊛⊛⊛

3 Slotskælderen hos Gitte Kik
This basement restaurant (open since 1910) is famous for its pickled herring and *schnapps*. ⊛ *Map K4* • *Fortunstræde 4* • *33 11 15 37* • *Open for lunch only* • *Closed Mon, Sun & Jul* • *www.slotskaelderen.dk* • ⊛⊛

4 Dan Turéll
One of the city's oldest cafés, it has a Parisian-style decor. ⊛ *Map K3* • *Store Regnegade 3* • *33 14 10 47* • *www.cafedanturell.dk* • ⊛⊛

5 Royal Smushi Café
This café has outdoor seating and a "smushi" menu, which combines traditional Danish *smørrebrød* with sushi. ⊛ *Map J4* • *Amagertorv 6* • *33 12 11 22* • *www. royalsmushicafe.dk* • ⊛⊛

6 Husmanns Vinstue
Once a stable, this comfy, wood-panelled lunch venue serves traditional fare *(see p67)*.

7 Hviids Vinstue
Copenhagen's oldest wine bar (established 1723) was one of H C Andersen's favourites. ⊛ *Map K4* • *Kongens Nytorv 19* • *33 15 10 64* • *www.hviidsvinstue.dk*

8 Charlie's Bar
Copenhagen's only Cask Marque pub, this serves 18 independent beers on tap. Danish brews include Hancock and Porse Guld. ⊛ *Map J4* • *Pilestræde 33* • *33 32 22 89*

9 Perch's Tea Room
Not much seems to have changed since 1834, when A C Perch started importing fine teas. Weighed on scales, the tea is brewed with reverence in the tea room on the first floor. ⊛ *Map J4* • *Kronprinsensgade 5* • *33 15 35 77* • *Closed Sun* • *www.perchs.dk*

10 Café Petersborg
Established in 1746, this restaurant serves traditional Danish fare. ⊛ *Map L2* • *Bredgade 76* • *33 12 50 16* • *Open daily (Sat–Sun lunch only)* • *Book ahead* • *www.cafe-petersborg.dk* • ⊛⊛

Left **Rosenborg Slot** Right **Marmorkirken**

Nørrebro, Østerbro and North of Gothersgade

OF THESE THREE NEIGHBOURHOODS, two are additions to the original Copenhagen site, which took up what is now called the "Inner City". Nørrebro, northwest of the Inner City, lies across the Dronning Louises Bro (Queen Louise's Bridge). Until the 19th century, this area was mainly farmland; today it is a lively, multicultural part of the city with plenty of bars, cafés and alternative shopping centres. Østerbro, slightly northeast of Nørrebro, has remained an uncluttered, suburban residential area since the 19th century. The train station, Østerport, was built in 1894–7 to help workers travel to the city centre, on the site of Copenhagen's fortified eastern gate. The area north of Gothersgade is part of the Inner City and takes in later parts of the original capital dating back to the Renaissance period.

Amalienborg

Sights

1 Assistens Kirkegård
2 Botanisk Have
3 Statens Museum for Kunst
4 Den Hirschsprungske Samling
5 Rosenborg Slot and Kongens Have
6 Davids Samling
7 Amalienborg
8 Marmorkirken
9 Designmuseum Danmark
10 Frihedsmuseet

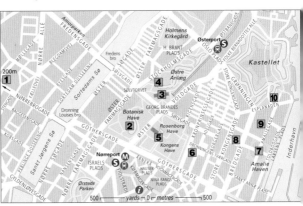

Preceding pages: **Christmas at Tivoli, the Chinese Pagoda.**

Assistens Kirkegård
If you are not a devoted fan of dead famous Danes, this cemetery may not be top of your list. However, it is a wonderful place to relax or take a romantic walk. The churchyard is beautiful and is located in the gritty Nørrebro district. ✆ *Map C3*
• *Kapelvej* • *35 37 19 17* • *Open Apr–Sep: 7am–10pm daily; Oct–Mar: 7am–7pm daily* • *www.assistens.dk*

Botanisk Have
Among the prettiest outdoor spaces in the city, these gardens are studded with lakes, bridges and lovely flowerbeds. Climb the winding staircase for a great view of exotic trees below. The grounds are also home to three museums which cover botany, geology and zoology.
✆ *Map H2–J2* • *Gothersgade 128; Øster Farimagsgade 2C* • *Open May–Sep: 8:30am–6pm daily; Oct–Apr: 8:30am–4pm daily* • *www.botanik.snm.ku.dk*

Statens Museum for Kunst
The National Gallery has an impressive collection of both national and international art, including works by the Old Masters and popular modern icons such as Matisse and Picasso *(see pp22–3)*.

Statens Museum for Kunst

Den Hirschsprungske Samling
This small art museum is situated just behind the National Gallery and displays the collection of tobacco magnate Heinrich Hirsch-sprung, given to the nation in 1902. Housed in a 19th-century building, the large collection is fittingly dedicated to 19th- and early 20th-century Danish art, including works by painters of the "Golden Age" and the North Jutland colony of Skagen painters, known for their bright colours and luminous treatment of light. Contemporary furniture is also displayed in the museum.
✆ *Map J1* • *Stockholmsgade 20* • *35 42 03 36* • *Open 11am–4pm Tue–Sun* • *Adm for adults; free Wed, free with Copenhagen Card* • *www.hirschsprung.dk*

Botanisk Have

5 Rosenborg Slot and Kongens Have

Rosenborg Castle and the King's Garden are among the city's highlights, especially on sunny days when the park is full of people and entertainment. Rosenborg Slot was built in 1606–34 on what was then the outskirts of the city. Today it is the only castle in the city centre that has not succumbed to fire. As a result, little has changed about the structure since the time the royal family inhabited it in the 17th and 18th centuries *(see pp14–15)*.

6 Davids Samling

This museum holds the lovely private art collection that belonged to Supreme Court barrister and art lover, C L David. The superb Islamic collection is the largest in Scandinavia, and includes a fine range of Islamic art and artifacts from the 8th to the 19th centuries. There is also a collection of European decorative arts from the 18th and 19th centuries. Set in an elegant, 19th-century town house, it is interesting to see the exhibits in a contemporaneous setting. *Map K3 • Kronprinsessegade 30–32 • 33 73 49 49 • Open 10am–5pm Tue–Sun (to 9pm Wed) • www.davidmus.dk*

7 Amalienborg

If you wish to look around inside the royal palaces, you need to visit on a weekend in summer. If you are unable to do so, you can only visit certain parts of the palace that have been set up as a museum. Either way, the Amalienborg complex is worth looking at from the outside. The palaces were built as an important part of the 18th-century aristocratic district Frederiksstaden and are very different from the narrow streets and houses of the old quarter. When it was first built, it was visually linked to the Marble Church *(see below)*; the modern Opera House *(see pp90–91)* and the construction across the harbour on Holmen offer a contemporary visual contrast *(see pp20–21)*.

8 Marmorkirken

Standing close to Amalienborg is the splendid Marmorkirken (Marble Church), a part of the great architectural design for Frederiksstaden. However, plans for its construction were so extravagant that finances ran out and work was abandoned in 1770. For more than a century, it stood as a picturesque ruin before being rescued and financed by a Danish industrialist, and

Amalienborg

Designmuseum Danmark

in 1894 the church was finally completed *(see pp20–21).*

Designmuseum Danmark

The National Museum of Art and Design is housed in a magnificent 18th-century Rococo building that was formerly Denmark's first hospital. The collection comprises everything from Danish-designed colanders and cardboard chairs to posters, textiles and Chinese decorative arts. The garden, Grønnegård, has its own summer theatre. Buy a picnic basket from the museum café to eat under the linden trees. Ⓢ *Map L2 • Bredgade 68 • 33 18 56 56 • Open 11am–5pm Tue–Sun (until 9pm Wed) • Adm for adults; free with Copenhagen Card • www.designmuseum.dk*

Frihedsmuseet

The Danish Resistance Museum pays tribute to, and tells the stories of, the people who lived in Denmark during the German occupation (1940–45). It explores their daily lives and the resistance activities that they undertook – from underground newspapers and radio stations to sabotage and the rescue of virtually every Jew in Denmark from under the noses of the Germans. The museum is currently closed due to fire damage. Ⓢ *Map L2 • Churchill-parken 7 • 33 47 39 21 • www.natmus.dk*

Walking Tour

Morning

Start your day at the **Den Hirschsprungske Samling** *(see p75)* museum, among the Impressionistic paintings of the Danish Skagen colony of painters. Then cross the gardens to the impressive **Statens Museum for Kunst** *(see 75);* take an audio guide to learn about the displays.

Afternoon

For lunch, stop over at either the museum café or the **Botanisk Have** *(see p75)* café, depending upon the weather. The gardens are a great place for a picnic, too. Don't forget to visit the palm house. Heading out from the gate on Øster Voldgade, cross over to **Rosenborg Slot.** You can spend a few enjoyable hours here, visiting the castle, the crown jewels and strolling through the gardens. Then, leave from the Kronprinsessegade gate and pop into the **Davids Samling** museum for some Islamic art. Walk down Dronningens Tværgade, take a left onto Bredgade and walk right up to **Marmorkirken**. If you are here by 3pm, take a tour up the tower. Right in front of the church is the **Amalienborg Palace Square**. Take a walk through it to the pretty banks of the harbour and see the **Opera House** *(see p8)* across the water. If you are up for a 20-minute walk, head towards **The Little Mermaid** *(see p78),* passing the distinctive **Gefionspringvandet** *(see p78)* and **Frihedsmuseet** (temporarily closed). To get back to town, hop on to the No 26 bus from Folke Bernadottes Allé.

Left **Gefionspringvandet** Right **Kastellet**

Best of the Rest

1 Gefionspringvandet
A dramatic sight, this bronze statue represents the tale of goddess Gefion ploughing enough land to create the island of Zealand (see p37). 🔉 Map M2

2 Medicinsk Museion
The Medical Museum of Copenhagen University has exhibits (some gruesome) dating back to the 18th century. 🔉 Map L2 • Bredgade 62 • 35 32 38 00 • Open noon–4pm Wed–Fri & Sun • Guided tour in English 2pm Wed–Fri, 1:30pm Sun • Adm for adults • www.museion.ku.dk

3 The Little Mermaid (Den Lille Havfrue)
This statue of the heroine of Andersen's fairy tale, *The Little Mermaid*, perched on a rock in the harbour, has been staring out to sea since 1913. 🔉 Map M1 • Langelinie

4 Amaliehaven
Filled with box hedges and fountains, this modern park lies to the east of Amalienborg, facing the harbour with views of the Opera House (see p21).

5 Kastellet
This pentagram-shaped fortress was built as protection against the Swedes, but only ever used against the English in 1807. 🔉 Map L1 • 33 47 95 00 • Only grounds open to visitors

6 Kastelskirken
The military church at Kastellet has been holding services since the 17th century. 🔉 Map L1 • Kastellet • 33 15 65 58 • Open 8am–6pm Mon–Fri • Some free Sunday concerts spring & autumn

7 St Alban's Church
Denmark's only Anglican church is a Neo-Gothic building from 1885. 🔉 Map M2 • Churchillparken 11 • 33 11 85 18 • Open to visitors in summer, 10am–4pm Mon–Fri • www.st-albans.dk

8 Kongelige Afstøbningssamling
The Royal Cast Collection is heralded on the harbour with a replica of Michelangelo's statue of *David*. 🔉 Map M2 • Toldbodgade 40 • 33 74 84 84 • Open 10am–4pm Tue, 2–5pm Sun • Free guided tours 3pm last Sun of the month (in Danish)

9 Alexander Nevsky Kirke
This Russian Orthodox church (1883) was a gift from Tsar Alexander III to celebrate his marriage to the Danish Princess Marie Dagmar. 🔉 Map L3 • Bredgade 53 • 33 13 60 46 • Open 11:30am–1:30pm

10 Fælledparken
Copenhagen's largest park is where the city gathers for the annual 1 May celebrations. 🔉 Map D2

Around Town – Nørrebro, Østerbro and North of Gothersgade

78

Price Categories		
For a three-course meal for one without alcohol, including taxes and extra charges.	ⓚ	up to 200 Dkr
	ⓚⓚ	200–300
	ⓚⓚⓚ	300–400
	ⓚⓚⓚⓚ	400–500
	ⓚⓚⓚⓚⓚ	over 500 Dkr

Restaurant Zeleste

🔟 Restaurants and Cafés

1 Restaurant Zeleste
This charming restaurant with a cosy interior serves good Continental-Danish fusion food. ⓢ *Map L4 • Store Strandstræde 6 • 33 16 06 06 • www.zeleste.dk • ⓚⓚⓚ*

2 Ida Davidsen
Excellent *smørrebrød* (open sandwiches) are on offer here, with an array of toppings. ⓢ *Map K3 • Store Kongensgade 70 • 33 91 36 55 • Open for lunch only • Closed Sat–Sun & Jul • www.idadavidsen.dk • ⓚⓚⓚ*

3 Salt Bar and Restaurant
Set inside an airy, 18th-century granary, this elegant bar and restaurant serves cocktails and French-Danish cuisine. ⓢ *Map L3 • Toldbodgade 24–8 • 33 74 14 44 • www.saltrestaurant.dk • ⓚⓚⓚⓚ*

4 Café Oscar
A rather conservative café with a great outdoor area, it has retained its classic decor over the decades. ⓢ *Map L3 • Bredgade 58 • 33 12 50 10 • www.cafeoscar.dk • ⓚⓚ*

5 Pussy Galore's Flying Circus
A Nørrebro favourite serving breakfasts, sandwiches and burgers. ⓢ *Map D3 • Skt Hans Torv 30, Nørrebro • 35 37 68 00 • www.pussygalore.dk • ⓚ*

6 Grønbech & Churchill
Michelin-starred fare that includes liquorice-laced bread, black Danish lobster and chocolate and honey mousse. Booking ahead is recommended (see p48).

7 Orangeriet Kongens Have
This elegant orangery in the park offers open sandwiches during the day and light seasonal dishes in the evening. ⓢ *Map K3 • Kronprinsessegade 13 • 33 11 13 07 • Open 11:30am–midnight Mon–Sat, noon–4pm Sun • www.restaurant-orangeriet.dk • ⓚⓚⓚⓚ*

8 Bopa
Serves a hearty brunch and café lunch (burgers, moussaka, etc.), and cocktails in the evening. ⓢ *Map E1 • Bopa Plads, Løgstørgade 8 • 35 43 05 66 • www.cafebopa.dk • ⓚⓚ*

9 Fischer
This tiny Italian restaurant is a favourite with local restaurant critics. Booking essential. ⓢ *Map E2 • Victor Borges Plads 12 • 35 42 39 64 • Open 5:30pm–10pm Mon–Wed, noon–midnight Thu–Fri, 10:30am–10pm Sat–Sun • www.hosfischer.dk • ⓚⓚⓚⓚ*

10 Kate's Joint
This popular eatery offers cheap dishes with South American, Indonesian and Caribbean influences. ⓢ *Map C4 • Blågårdsgade 12 • 35 37 44 96 • Open dinner only • ⓚ*

Left **Eco Ego** Right **Tage Andersen Boutique & Museum**

 Shopping

1 Tage Andersen Boutique & Museum

Run by flower artist and designer Tage Andersen, this flower shop, gallery and museum is full of lovely and unique arrangements. 🌐 *Map K4 • Ny Adelgade 12 • 33 93 09 13 • www.tage-andersen.com*

2 Divaen og Krudtuglen

Bright clothes and shoes for kids and mums alike, as well as trays of cute, inexpensive toys. 🌐 *Map C3 • Elmegade 22 • 26 71 59 68 • www.millou.dk*

3 Susanne Juul

Suppliers of hats to royalty and celebrities. 🌐 *Map K3 • Store Kongensgade 14 • 33 32 25 22 • Closed Mon & Sun • www.susannejuul.dk*

4 Normann Copenhagen

This vast warehouse housed in an old cinema is filled with designer furniture, clothes and interior design items. 🌐 *Map E2 • Østerbrogade 70 • 35 27 05 40 • www.normann-copenhagen.com*

5 Eco Ego

Denmark's first fair-trade, organic lifestyle shop sells everything from shoes and skincare products to games. 🌐 *Map H3 • Nørre Farimagsgade 82 • 32 12 06 12 • www.ecoego.dk*

6 Baan Suan

Visit this store for pretty, feminine clothing with embroidery, flower motifs and polka dots. Do also check out their varied range of colourful, ethnic jewellery, sunglasses and bags. 🌐 *Map C3 • Elmegade 18 • 35 39 19 40*

7 Nyhavns Glaspusteri

This charming glass gallery is where glass-blower Christian Edwards sculpts and sells his creations. 🌐 *Map L4 • Toldbodgade 4 • 33 13 01 34 • www.copenhagenglass.dk*

8 Klædebo

Exquisite, handmade silk dresses now hang in this small boutique. Once a cheese shop, the interior is still lined with the original tiling. 🌐 *Map C3 • Blågårdsgade 3 • 35 36 05 27 • Closed Mon*

9 Juice

This was one of the first trendy clothing boutiques to be set up in Nørrebro. 🌐 *Map C3 • Elmegade 17 • 35 36 15 58*

10 Mondo Kaos

New versions of vintage clothes, including retro 1950s-style dresses, are on the racks of this colourful rockabilly boutique. 🌐 *Map C3 • Birkegade 1 • 60 95 11 36 • www.mondokaos.dk*

Left **Rust** Right **Gefährlich**

🔟 Nightlife

Props Coffee Shop
The relaxed ambience of this Berlin-inspired bar makes it a good spot to enjoy locally brewed beer. 🚭 *Map C3 • Blågårdsgade 5 • 35 36 99 55*

Gefährlich
This is one of the most popular bars in the area. It also has a good restaurant and live music. 🚭 *Map C3 • Fælledvej 7 • 35 24 13 24 • Closed Mon & Sun • www.gefahrlich.dk*

Rust
Tune into Copenhagen's alternative music scene live at this trendy bar. There is a night-club in the basement. 🚭 *Map C3 • Guldbergsgade 8 • 35 24 52 00 • Night-club: min age Wed–Thu 18, Fri–Sat 20 • Open 11pm–4am Wed, 8pm–5am Fri–Sat • www.rust.dk*

Café Pavillonen
Located beside a lake, this lovely, 18th-century-style rotunda holds open-air salsa with DJs in summer. 🚭 *Map D2 • Edel Sauntes Allé 22, Østerbro • 35 38 73 83 • Open Apr–Oct from noon • www.cafepavillonen.dk*

Empire Bio Cinema
This comfortable arts cinema holds good programmes and has a cosy bar and café area. 🚭 *Map C3 • Guldbergsgade 29F • 35 36 00 36 • www.empirebio.dk*

Bodega
Popular and reasonably priced, this pre-clubbing venue serves good bar food. It also has a dance floor; DJ sessions are held on Fridays and Saturdays and kick off at 9pm. 🚭 *Map C3 • Kapelvej 1 • 35 39 07 07 • www.bodega.dk*

Park Diskotek
This black-walled, pink-curtained club specializes in R&B and house music. 🚭 *Map E2 • Østerbrogade 79 • 70 33 32 22 • Open 11pm–5am Fri–Sat • Dress code • www.parkcafe.dk*

Pussy Galore's Flying Circus
A hangout for Crown Prince Frederik in his bachelor days, this trendy club serves hamburgers, salads and cocktails (see p79).

The Oak Room
This tiny cocktail bar consists of one long narrow room. Popular with the locals. 🚭 *Map C3 • Birkegade 10 • 38 60 38 60 • Open Wed–Sat • www.oakroom.dk*

Mexibar
This cosy, Mexican-inspired bar serves good cocktails. The staff are friendly. 🚭 *Map C3 • Elmegade 27 • 35 37 77 66 • Closed Sun*

Left **Frederiksberg Slot** Right **Zoologisk Have**

Vesterbro and Frederiksberg

VESTERBRO AND FREDERIKSBERG *lie side by side to the southwest and west of the Inner City. In the 19th century both Vesterbro and Frederiksberg were outside the city walls; this was when Tivoli was built on Vesterbro's extreme edge. Vesterbro was formerly an area where the poor lived in humble two-room flats with no running water, and included a red-light district. Although the area retains an edginess shared only by the Nørrebro district, much of it has been regenerated. Today, you will find a thriving underground culture, designer fashion outlets and a multicultural population. The popular, former meat-packing district Kødbyen and the more outlying Carlsberg Byen, on the site of the old brewery, are cultural neighbourhoods in themselves. In contrast, prosperous former village Frederiksberg is still a fairly tranquil, up-market residential area, and remains an independent municipality that is not officially part of Copenhagen.*

Sights

1 Københavns Museum
2 Frederiksberg Have
3 Zoologisk Have
4 Radisson Blu Royal Hotel
5 Carlsberg Brewery
6 Frederiksberg Slot
7 Tycho Brahe Planetarium
8 Storm P Museet
9 Bakkehusmuseet
10 Cisternerne – Museet for Moderne Glaskunst

Storm P Museet

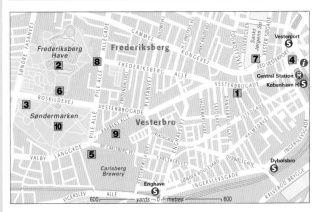

Around Town – Vesterbro and Frederiksberg

82

Københavns Museum

The City Museum takes you on a journey through the city's history, right from its small beginnings on the island of Slotsholmen in the 12th century. There are many interesting exhibits, including atmospheric reconstructions, a slide show of Copenhagen through the ages and sights of a medieval town. A large model of medieval Copenhagen gives a clear view of the buildings that existed then and the area that was covered by the city.

⊗ *Map C5 • Vesterbrogade 59 • 33 21 07 72 • Open 10am–5pm daily • Adm for adults; Fri free • www.bymuseum.dk*

Frederiksberg Have

Frederiksberg Gardens surround Frederiksberg Slot *(see p84)* and make up a lovely green area that recalls the castle's aristocratic past. Between 1798 and 1802, the original Baroque gardens were landscaped to conform with the Romantic style of the English garden. Several buildings here date back to the Golden Age (1800–50), including the Chinese Pavilion, the Neo-Classical Møstings House, the Swiss House (a cottage built for the royal family to have tea) and the colonnaded Apis Temple.

⊗ *Map A5 • Open 6am–sundown daily*

Frederiksberg Have

Zoologisk Have

Open 365 days a year, this zoo makes for a lovely day out. Here you will find a wide variety of animals from tigers to monkeys (including the tiny, endangered Golden Lion Tamarins). Visit the Norman Foster-designed elephant house, where two large domes in the roof flood the stables with daylight, providing a great place to see these magnificent creatures.

⊗ *Map A5 • Roskildevej 32 • 72 20 02 00 • Open Apr–May & Sep: 10am–5pm Mon–Fri, 10am–6pm Sat–Sun; Jun & last 2 weeks of Aug: 10am–6pm daily; Jul & first 2 weeks of Aug: 10am–8pm daily; Oct–Mar: 10am–4pm daily (to 5pm Oct) • Adm; free with Copenhagen Card • www.zoo.dk*

Radisson Blu Royal Hotel

The city's tallest building, this 20-storey tower-block hotel, designed by architect Arne Jacobsen, represents the cutting-edge design of the 1950s. About the radical design, Arne Jacobsen said, "They call it the 'punch card', and it's funny, because that is what it looks like when the windows are open on a hot summer's day." ⊗ *Map G5 • Hammerichsgade 1 • 33 42 60 00 • www.radisson.com*

Københavns Museum

Carlsberg Brewery

Carlsberg Brewery

The Carlsberg Brewery, established by Jacob Jacobsen in 1847, offers an exhibition and tour charting the brewery's history and its brands (including a collection of over 16,000 beer bottles from around the world). Carlsberg is no longer produced on the premises (only Jacobsen Brewery survives), but the rich history of brewing can still be discovered here. Other parts of the brewery have been developed into a cultural quarter, Carlsberg Byen, with art galleries, an adventure park, Europe's largest dance centre (DANCE-hallerne) and the Fotografisk Center. ◈ *Map A6 • Gamle Carlsberg Vej 11 • 33 27 10 20 • Open 10am–5pm daily • Adm (free for under-6s); free with Copenhagen Card • www.visitcarlsberg.dk*

Frederiksberg Slot

Not to be mistaken for Frederiksborg Slot in Hillerød *(see p98)*, this castle was originally a 17th-century pavilion built by Frederik IV as a royal court. As it was rather small, it was extended several times after its construction. The building that stands here today (built in 1829) has an Italian-ate, Baroque architecture and is used as a training school for army cadets. ◈ *Map A5 • Closed to the public*

Tycho Brahe Planetarium

The permanent exhibition at the Planetarium includes displays on the natural sciences, astronomy and space travel. However, one of the biggest attractions is the IMAX cinema; visitors are blown away by the enormous, high-quality images on the 1,000-sq-m (over 10,500-sq-ft) dome screen. Films cover topics like astronomy and space research, and virtually transport you to another world. ◈ *Map C5 • Gammel Kongevej 10 • 33 12 12 24 • Open noon–7:40pm Mon, 9:30am–7:40pm Tue–Thu, 10:45am–8.50pm Fri–Sat, 10:45am–7:40pm Sun • Adm (includes exhibition and film showing); free with Copenhagen Card • Min age for films: 3 years • www.tycho.dk*

Storm P Museet

This small museum is a delightful find. It is dedicated to the whimsical and satirical wit of the Danish cartoonist Storm P, whose distinctive style seems to recall the social realism of the late 19th and early 20th centuries, such as the styles of Daumier, Toulouse-Lautrec and Degas. His sense of humour comes through brilliantly in the dialogues of his characters. If you speak Danish, you will derive great enjoyment from these cartoons. However, non-Danish speakers will also enjoy the displays visually. ◈ *Map A5 • Frederiksberg Runddel • 38 86 05 00 • Open 10am–4pm Tue–Sun • Adm for adults; free with Copenhagen Card • www.stormp.dk*

Bakkehusmuseet

Formerly, the home of 19th-century Golden Age literary personalities Kamma and Lyhne Rahbek, this old house is now a cultural museum. Four rooms have retained their original decor (1802–30), and two are dedicated

If the Carlsberg Brewery has given you a taste for beer, head for Charlie's Bar, see p71; for microbreweries, see p53.

Jacob Jacobsen

Lager beer was unheard of in Copenhagen until news arrived of "Bavarian beers" being made by ageing (lagering). Jacob Jacobsen (1811–87), who made beer in the ale-making tradition, left at once for Munich to get some lager yeast. In 1847, he introduced his first lager and set up the Carlsberg Brewery (named after his son). Carlsberg is now one of the world's best lagers.

to the Danish poets Johannes Ewald and Adam Oehlenschläger. You will also find a variety of H C Andersen memorabilia here. ◉ *Map B6 • Rahbeks Allé 23, Frederiksberg • 33 31 43 62 • Open 11am–4pm Tue–Sun • Adm • www. bakkehusmuseet.dk*

🔟 Cisternerne – Museet for Moderne Glaskunst

This remarkable, candle-lit glass museum is intriguing not only for its stained-glass exhibits by artists like Per Kirkeby and Robert Jacobsen, but also for its location. Set inside the cave-like water cistern of an old supply plant, it lies beneath the grassy lawns of Frederiksberg Have and has numerous thin stalactites on the ceiling.
◉ *Map A6 • Søndermarken 25 • 33 21 93 10 • Open 11am–5pm Tue–Sun • Closed Dec–Feb • Adm; free for under-18s • www.cisternerne.dk*

Tycho Brahe Planetarium

A Walk Around Vesterbro

🕐 Start at the central station, Hovedbanegård, and see the Frihedsstøtten or "pillar of freedom" (1792). Continue down Vester-brogade and take a left at Reventlowgade, then a right on to Istedgade until you reach the old red-light district. Walk up to **Halmtorvet**, a former cattle market now full of cafés and restaurants, known as Den Brune Kødby (brown meat city). The large building opposite is **Øksnehallen**, Vesterbro's biggest cultural exhibition space. From here, stroll on to the blue-painted complex, **Den Hvide Kødby** (white meat city), now a lively cluster of bars, galleries and clubs. Head back to Halmtorvet and take a right on Skyde-banegade. At the end of the street is a wall that protected inhabitants from shooting practice that took place in the gardens on the other side. Go through the gate in the wall, through the park to the **Københavns Museum** *(see p83)*. Take a look at the city model outside and, if you wish, visit the museum. Continue along Vesterbrogade, taking a left onto Oehlenschläg-ersgade, where you will find an extraordinary mosaic-covered bar created by the late Nigerian-born artist Manuel Tafat. Head back to Vesterbrogade for lunch at **Les Trois Cochons** *(see p87)* on Værnedamsvej, or continue down Oehlen-schlægersgade until you reach the trendy bars and boutiques on Istedgade. You could also stop over for lunch or a drink at **Café Bang & Jensen** at 130 *(see p87)*. Spend the rest of the afternoon browsing through the stylish shops.

Left **Designer Zoo** Right **Meyers Deli**

🔟 Shopping

Danefæ
This popular Danish clothing brand opened its Vesterbro branch in 2013. Specializes in quirky, brightly coloured separates with bold motifs.
🇸 *Map C6 • Istedgade 83 • 61 30 84 85 • www.danefae.dk*

Donn Ya Doll
Donn Ya Doll opened in the techno-era 1990s and has retained something of a space age look. It stocks hip and original clothing and accessories, some designed by the shop's owner.
🇸 *Map C5 • Istedgade 55 • 33 22 66 35*

Girlie Hurly
This shop is filled with quirky, colourful items for girls, from bags and candles to lamps and crockery. 🇸 *Map C6 • Istedgade 99 • 33 24 22 41*

Rockahula
This intriguing little boutique is dedicated to all things 1950s and rockabilly, including a children's line. 🇸 *Map C6 • Istedgade 91 • 26 23 42 67 • www.rockahula.dk*

Klaus Samsøe
With meat hooks in the ceiling, this store is the offbeat brother of menswear designer Samsøe's city branches. 🇸 *Map B5 • Vesterbrogade 178*

Tiger Lily
This tiny vintage clothes shop sells funky, designer second-hand clothes in retro Bohemian styles.

🇸 *Map C5 • Værnedamsvej 11 • 44 61 22 04 • Closed Wed & Sun*

Designer Zoo
This is a mecca for the design conscious, with clothing, ceramics, jewellery and even furniture by in-house designers.
🇸 *Map B5 • Vesterbrogade 137 • 33 24 94 93 • www.dzoo.dk*

Meyers Deli
Claus Meyer helped kickstart the Nordic kitchen movement and his deli provides Noma-style food, from relishes to ready meals, that you can take home.
🇸 *Map B5 • Gammel Kongevej 107 • 33 25 45 95 • Open until 8pm daily • www.meyersdeli.dk*

Værnedamsvej
This gourmet food street, nicknamed Little Paris, has butchers, fishmongers, wine and chocolate shops. 🇸 *Map C5*

Le Marché Deli Takeaway
Stop here for home-cooked, take-away meals. Changing evening menu. 🇸 *Map C5 • Værnedamsvej 2 • 33 31 39 35 • www.cofoco.dk*

Café Lindevang

Price Categories

For a three-course meal for one without alcohol, including taxes and extra charges.

⊗	up to 200 Dkr
⊗⊗	200–300
⊗⊗⊗	300–400
⊗⊗⊗⊗	400–500
⊗⊗⊗⊗⊗	over 500 Dkr

☉10 Dining

1 Café Lindevang

Café Lindevang is known for its generous portions. Meatballs and herring are accompanied by a range of *schnapps*. ⊗ *Map C5 • Sløjfen 6 (Lindevang metro stop) • 38 34 38 34 • Closed Sun • www.cafelindevang.dk • ⊗⊗*

2 Café Bang & Jensen

This ex-pharmacy is now a popular café-bar. Fun cocktails and good music make for lively nights. ⊗ *Map C6 • Istedgade 130 • 33 25 53 18 • www.bangogjensen.dk • ⊗⊗*

3 Les Trois Cochons

Aptly named ("the three pigs" in French), this restaurant is inside an old butcher's shop. It serves great southern French food at reasonable prices. ⊗ *Map C5 • Værnedamsvej 10 • 33 31 70 55 • Book ahead • ⊗⊗⊗*

4 Cofoco

Delicious, reasonably priced French-Danish food is served at a long communal table. ⊗ *Map C5 • Abel Cathrines Gade 7 • 33 13 60 60 • Book ahead • ⊗⊗*

5 Sticks 'n' Sushi

Try the mouthwatering sushi, sashimi or yakitori at this friendly Euro-Japanese café-bar. ⊗ *Map C6 • Istedgade 62 • 33 23 73 04 • www.sushi.dk • ⊗⊗*

6 Famo

Co-owned by the former head chef of Era Ora *(see p48)*, this restaurant serves inexpensive, good-quality Italian cuisine. ⊗ *Map C5 • Saxogade 3 • 33 23 22 50 • Book ahead • www.famo.dk • ⊗⊗⊗⊗*

7 Frederiks Have

Housed in a 19th-century building with a covered courtyard, Frederiks Have serves Swedish and Danish specialities. ⊗ *Map A4 • Smallegade 41 • 38 88 33 35 • Closed Sun • www.frederikshave.dk • ⊗⊗⊗⊗*

8 Mother

This hip pizzeria is known for its high-quality sourdough bases and freshly made classic toppings. ⊗ *Map C6 • Høkerboderne 9–15 • 22 27 58 98 • www.mother.dk • ⊗*

9 Formel B

Enjoy French-influenced food made with farm-fresh ingredients on the terrace, or in the candle-lit interiors. ⊗ *Map B5 • Vesterbrogade 182 • 33 25 10 66 • Closed Sun • Book ahead • www.formel-b.dk • ⊗⊗⊗⊗⊗*

10 Restaurant Klubben

This pub is famous for its large portions of Danish food. ⊗ *Map B5 • Enghavevej 4 • 33 31 40 15 • www.restaurant-klubben.dk • ⊗⊗*

Left **Christiania** Right **Overgaden Neden Vandet**

Christianshavn and Holmen

AFTER THE INNER CITY, *this settlement on the island of Amager is the oldest part of Copenhagen. There is some evidence that it was inhabited during the Stone Age. In 1521, Christian II invited Dutch gardeners (whom he held in high regard) to this fertile area to plant and run market gardens. A century later, Christian IV built fortifications in the area and a town on an island at the north end. Soon, the Amagerbro bridge was built to connect the two islands; the Knippelsbro bridge stands in its place today. The canals of Christianshavn, lined with houseboats and pretty 17th-century houses, are a special attraction in this charming area that is reminiscent of Amsterdam. Holmen, to the north of Christianshavn, is made up of three man-made islets. It was created in 1690 as a naval area with dockyards, accommodation and*

offices; the navy remained here until 1989. Since then, the area has seen an increase in public spaces, forums, residential housing, art and design schools, and is also home to its star attraction, the impressive Opera House.

Operaen

🔟 Sights

1. **Christiania**
2. **Christians Kirke**
3. **Vor Frelsers Kirke**
4. **Inderhavnen**
5. **Holmen and Refshaleøen**
6. **Overgaden Neden Vandet & Overgaden Oven Vandet**
7. **North Atlantic House**
8. **Orlogsmuseet**
9. **Operaen**
10. **Gammel Dok**

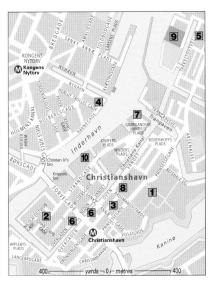

Christians Kirke

1 Christiania
In the 1970s, this rebellious squatters' enclave, set up in abandoned military barracks, was an inspirational new society with its own set of laws, readily available drugs and no tax system. The area has now become a bit more conventional; the inhabitants have been paying taxes since 1994, and the stands that sold drugs on Pusher Street closed down in 2004. In 2011, residents and the State came to an agreement giving Christiania residents the right to buy, making the squat official for the first time. There are no actual sights but many hippy hangouts. ✎ *Map M5*

2 Christians Kirke
Originally known as Frederiks Kirke, this interesting yellow-brick church was renamed Christians Kirke (after Christian IV, founder of this part of Copenhagen) in 1901. It was built between 1755 and 1759 in the Rococo style by Nicolai Eigtved, Frederik V's master architect. The interior looks almost like a theatre, with second-level seating galleries and the altar taking the place of the stage. The elegant tower was added by Eigtved's son-in-law, G D Anthon, 10 years after the church was built. ✎ *Map K6 • Strandgade 1 • 32 54 15 76 • Open 9am–4pm Tue–Fri • www.christianskirke.com*

3 Vor Frelsers Kirke
This magnificent Baroque church was built (1682–96) by the Dutch-Norwegian architect Lambert van Haven in the form of a Greek cross. Its trademark twisted tower was added 50 years later (1749–52). Inside the church, look out for the putti-covered font, presented in 1702 by Frederik IV's morganatic wife who hoped to have children. Unfortunately, she died in 1704 during childbirth and the baby died nine months later. Don't miss the marvellous altarpiece, which represents God as the Sun and depicts the scene in the garden of Gethsemane, when Christ prayed that he should not die on the cross. The organ, built like a three-storey house, rests on two elephants. ✎ *Map L6 • Sankt Annae Gade 29 • 32 54 68 83 • Open 11am–3:30pm daily • Tower: Open Mar–May & Oct–Nov: 10am–4pm Mon–Sat, 10:30am–4pm Sun; Jun–Sep: 10am–7:30pm Mon–Sat, 10:30am–7:30pm Sun • Adm for tower; free with Copenhagen Card • www.vorfrelserskirke.dk*

4 Inderhavnen
Christianshavn is dominated by waterways. Its canals are tributaries of the Inner Harbour (Inderhavnen), which separates it from the rest of the city, eventually widening to become the Øresund (Sound). A harbour tour, usually from Nyhavn *(see p8)*, is a great way to appreciate the area. ✎ *Map J6–M4*

Around Town – Christianshavn and Holmen

Orlogsmuseet

Holmen and Refshaleøen

North of Christianshavn is Holmen and Refshaleøen, a former shipyard that is now the setting for outdoor activity centres for climbing, bungy jumping and paintball. Also here are innovative restaurants and a summertime beach bar, Halvandet. The site hosted the 2014 Eurovision Song contest. ✎ *Map M3*

Overgaden Neden Vandet & Overgaden Oven Vandet

These two cobbled streets lie on either side of the Christianshavns canal. Overgaden Neden Vandet ("upper street below the water") is the quayside that runs along the Sound side of the canal. It is lined with 17th-century buildings, one of which is the Era Ora restaurant *(see pp 48 & 93)*. Overgaden Oven Vandet ("upper street above the water") is also lined with 17th-century houses, including the Orlogmuseel *(see opposite)*. ✎ *Map L6–M5*

North Atlantic House

The North Atlantic House is a cultural centre for Iceland, Greenland and the Faroes. It is housed in an 18th-century warehouse, formerly the Greenlandic Trading Square, which hosts art displays and events. The Noma restaurant is also here *(see pp49 & 93)*. ✎ *Map M4 • Strandgade 91 • 32 83 37 00 • Open 10am–5pm Mon–Fri, noon–5pm Sat–Sun • Adm (free for under-11s and with Copenhagen Card) • www.nordatlantens.dk*

Orlogsmuseet

The Royal Danish Naval Museum, located in an area that was influenced by the navy and its docks for centuries, documents Danish naval history from 1669. There are beautiful, detailed models of ships and harbours, and a few reconstructions of important Danish sea battles. Some of the models were used as sailors' teaching aids, to show cadets how to strip and re-rig the sails. Most of the information is available in both Danish and English. The museum building (dating back to 1781) was originally used as a naval hospital and then as a state prison until the 1830s. ✎ *Map L5 • Overgaden Oven Vandet 58 • 33 11 60 37 • Open noon–4pm Tue–Sun • www. natmus.dk/orlogsmuseet*

Operaen

The Opera House was the first major public building to be built in the Holmen area after the

navy vacated the docks in 1979. Architect Henning Larsen emphasized its location near the water with large glass windows and no pillars on the ground floor. The interior has a maritime feel as well, with balconies, open spaces and white railings. The position of the Opera House caused controversy when it was built because it lies directly opposite the Amalienborg. The design of the Opera House was also the cause of some friction when its benefactor, Mærsk McKinney Møller, insisted that his own ideas be incorporated into the construction *(see p42).*
◈ *Map M3 • Ekvipagemestervej 10 • 33 69 69 69 • Guided tours available; call for times • www.kglteater.dk*

Gammel Dok

Gammel Dok ("Old Dock") was built in 1739, a time when the navy's ships moored along-side. The warehouse dates back to 1882 and now houses the Danish Architecture Centre. It holds exhibitions and provides a working space for young artists and architects who win scholarships to study here. A café on the first floor offers great views over the water. ◈ *Map L5 • Dansk Arkitektur Centre, Strandgade 27B • 32 57 19 30 • Open 10am–5pm (to 9pm Wed) • Adm for adults; free 5–9pm; free with Copenhagen Card • www.dac.dk*

Sightseeing from the water

Walking Tour

Morning

Start at the Knippelsbro Bridge. Built in 1937, the bridge takes its name from Hans Knip, the tollkeeper of the first bridge built here in the 17th century. Turn right to visit **Christians Kirke** on Strandgade *(see p89).* Then, retrace your steps and cross Torvegade, walking right up to the corner of Sankt Annæ Gade. At the corner is No 32 (built in 1622–4), said to be the oldest house in Christianshavn. Turn right and then left on to **Overgaden Oven Vandet** and walk along the canal. Pop inside the **Royal Danish Naval Museum** for a quick visit. If you are curious about **Christiania** *(see p89),* take a right down Brobergsgade, cross Prinsessegade and pass through the gate reading "you are now leaving the EU". If you are not going to the opera in the evening, continue along the canal-side and take a right turn at Bodenhoffs Plads, then a left onto Værftsbroen. Keep walking (or take the bus 66) towards the **Opera House**. Hop on a harbour bus *(see p8)* back to Knippelsbro for lunch at **Café Wilder** *(see p93)* on Wildersgade and head down Sankt Annæ Gade to visit **Vor Frelsers Kirke** *(see p89).*

Afternoon

Spend the afternoon shopping. If you are in the mood for a drink, there are cafés along the Christians-havns Kanal. Linger over supper at **L'Altro** on Torve-gade *(see p93)* or catch a performance at the **Opera House** (taking the bus 66 or the water bus from Knippelsbro).

Left **Mo Christianshavn** Right **Inblik**

🔟 Shopping

1 Mo Christianshavn
This shop and workshop is owned by Mo, a jewellery designer. ◎ *Map L5 • Torvegade 24 • 26 80 17 26 • Open Thu–Sat • www.mo.dk*

2 Bit Antik
This tiny shop is filled with pieces from Denmark's yester-years, including old dolls and doll houses, books, glasses, sculpture and porcelain. ◎ *Map L6 • Prinsess-egade 17B • 40 72 09 62 • Open 3–6pm Wed only • www.bitantik.dk*

3 Porte à Gauche
This trendy boutique offers Scandinavian designer wear for women. You will also find classic, exotic Julie Sandlau jewellery. ◎ *Map L5 • Torvegade 20 • 32 54 01 40 • www.porteagauche.dk*

4 Aurum
Some 20 international jewellers are represented at Aurum. Many materials, including precious stones, are used to create these unique pieces. ◎ *Map L6 • Wildersgade 26 • 25 30 00 11 • www.aurumcph.com*

5 Inblik
This delightful gift shop has an eclectic collection, including stylish lighters and gadgets, shoes and jewellery, children's games and unusual photo frames. ◎ *Map L5 • Torvegade 38 • 32 57 65 61*

6 Lagkagehuset
Well known for its breads, cakes and pastries, this bakery has a fine selection of goodies during Christmas. ◎ *Map L6 • Torvegade 45 • 32 57 36 07 • Open from 6am daily*

7 Pang Christianshavn
This shop sells gifts, clothes and shoes, as well as all kinds of kitschy items for the home in bright colours. ◎ *Map L6 • Sankt Annæ Gade 31 • 32 96 68 80 • www.pangchristianshavn.dk*

8 Hilbert København
Jewellery is made to order here by goldsmith Morten Hilbert. ◎ *Map L6 • Sankt Annæ Gade 24 • 33 93 53 01 • Closed Sat*

9 Cibi e Vini
This Italian delicatessen sells organic wine, fresh bread, pasta and meats. ◎ *Map L5 • Torvegade 28 • 32 57 77 98 • www.cibievini.dk*

10 Christiania Shop
In the same building as the Christiania art gallery, this shop sells Christiania souvenirs, the profits going towards keeping the Free State free. ◎ *Map M5 • Loppebygningen • 60 80 88 62*

Price Categories

For a three-course meal for one without alcohol, including taxes and extra charges.

⊛ up to 200 Dkr
⊛⊛ 200–300
⊛⊛⊛ 300–400
⊛⊛⊛⊛ 400–500
⊛⊛⊛⊛⊛ over 500 Dkr

Sofiekælderen

🔟 Cafés, Bars and Restaurants

1 Era Ora
One of the best Italian restaurants in Denmark, Era Ora offers warm service in a tranquil setting, delicious food and a vast wine list. ⊛ *Map L6 • Overgaden Neden Vandet 33B • 32 54 06 93 • Closed Sun • Book ahead • www.era-ora.dk* • ⊛⊛⊛⊛⊛

2 L'Altro
Relish homely Umbrian-Tuscan dishes in the relaxed atmosphere of this *antiristorante*, a 1950s Italian expression that means "to dine at home". ⊛ *Map L6 • Torvegade 62 • 32 54 54 06 • Closed Sun • www.laltro.dk* • ⊛⊛⊛⊛

3 Spiseloppen
Sample constantly changing menus from a truly international kitchen. ⊛ *Map F5 • Bådmandstræde 43 • 32 57 95 58 • Closed Mon • Book ahead • www.spiseloppen.dk* • ⊛⊛

4 Luna's Diner
Popular American-style diner in the heart of Christianshavn. Known for its burgers, breakfast specials and vegetarian options. ⊛ *Map L6 • Sankt Annæ Gade 5 • 32 54 20 00 • www.lunasdiner.dk* • ⊛⊛

5 Sofiekælderen
This café-bar is so close to the water, you could climb down to the boats moored alongside. Enjoy a night out at its famous bar and nightclub. ⊛ *Map L6 • Overgaden Oven Vandet 32 • 32 57 77 01 • Closed Sun • www.sofiekaelderen.dk* • ⊛⊛⊛

6 Café Wilder
Enjoy good French-Italian-inspired food and coffee at this café. ⊛ *Map L5 • Wildersgade 56 • 32 54 71 83 • www.cafewilder.dk* • ⊛⊛⊛

7 Noma
This award-winning restaurant serves gourmet cuisine made with seasonal Scandinavian produce. ⊛ *Map M5 • Strandgade 93 • 32 96 32 97 • Closed Sun–Mon • Book ahead • www.noma.dk* • ⊛⊛⊛⊛⊛

8 Rabes Have
Opened for local soldiers and sailors in 1632, this is the oldest pub in Copenhagen. ⊛ *Map K6 • Langebrogade 8 • 32 57 34 17 • Open until 5pm only • Closed Mon–Tue* • ⊛

9 Bastionen & Løven
Famous for brunch, but also good for a romantic evening. ⊛ *Map L6 • Christianshavns Voldgade 50 • 32 95 09 40 • www.bastionen-loven.dk* • ⊛⊛⊛

10 Oven Vande Café
Enjoy tasty salads, soups and paninis at this café. ⊛ *Map L5 • Overgaden Oven Vandet 44 • 32 95 96 02 • www.cafeovenvande.dk* • ⊛⊛

Left **Ordrupgaard** Right **Helsingør**

Beyond Copenhagen

ALTHOUGH COPENHAGEN ITSELF *will easily keep you entertained for several days, the area around the city offers many opportunities for days out. Roskilde and Helsingør provide a taste of Nordic history, from the Viking era to the founding of Copenhagen. Get a sense of medieval maritime defence of the Sound at Helsingør's Kronborg Slot and explore the royal lifestyle in the 17th and 18th centuries at Frederiksborg and Charlottenlund. Art- and literature-lovers can drop in at Arken, Louisiana, Ordrupgaard and the Karen Blixen Museet, home to internationally acclaimed collections. Frilandsmuseet and Den Blå Planet are a must-visit for kids.*

Frederiksborg Slot

Charlottenlund Slotshave

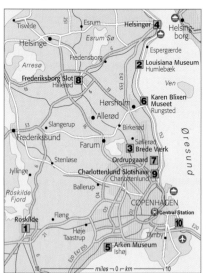

Sights

1. Roskilde
2. Louisiana Museum
3. Frilandsmuseet
4. Helsingør
5. Arken Museum for Moderne Kunst
6. Karen Blixen Museet
7. Ordrupgaard
8. Frederiksborg Slot
9. Charlottenlund Slotshave
10. Den Blå Planet

Preceding pages: **Interior of Den Sorte Diamant.**

Roskilde

Roskilde, a mere 25 minutes away from the city centre by train, makes for a fascinating day out. Older than Copenhagen itself, this was the original seat of Absalon, Bishop of Roskilde and founder of the city. Here you will find a medieval cathedral, a royal burial site and the wonderful Viking Ship Museum, which offers fjord trips on replica Viking longboats *(see p100)*.

Louisiana Museum

This should be high on the list for modern art enthusiasts. The museum houses an impressive selection of works by international artists like Picasso, Alberto Giacometti and Francis Bacon, and Danish masters like Asger Jorn and Per Kirkeby. There is also a children's wing, which offers art-related activities for kids between 3 and 16 years (call for details). The coastal location, extensive sculpture park and excellent café make the museum even more appealing *(see also p101)*. 🔍 *Map B2 • Gammel Strandvej 13, Humlebæk • 49 19 07 19 • Open 11am–10pm Tue–Fri, 11am–6pm Sat–Sun • Adm for adults; free for under-18s, free with Copenhagen Card • Guided tours available in English; book ahead • Dis access • www.louisiana.dk*

Roskilde

Frilandsmuseet

Part of the Nationalmuseet *(see pp26–7)*, Denmark's Open Air Museum brings history alive through working exhibits from the period 1650–1940. Explore farms, windmills and a cooperative village. There are old Danish breeds of livestock here, including pigs, sheep and geese. Next to the site's northern entrance on I. C. Modewegs Vej is Brede Værk, a former textile mill that has been converted into an interactive museum charting Denmark's industrial revolution. 🔍 *Map B2 • Konggevejen 100, Kongens Lyngby • 41 20 64 55 • Open May–mid-Oct: 10am–4pm Tue–Sun (5pm Jul & first 2 wks of Aug • Free • natmus.dk/en/the-open-air-museum*

Helsingør

In the 1400s, this harbour town levied tax on all sea traffic that passed through the Sound, which is just 4 km (2½ miles) wide at this point. Apart from a pretty medieval centre, other sights include the 16th-century castle, Kronborg Slot, the Carmelite monastery and the Maritime Museum of Denmark *(see p102)*.

Café in Louisiana Museum

5 Arken Museum for Moderne Kunst

This wonderful museum houses a rotating permanent collection of contemporary international and Danish art, along with temporary exhibitions. The white, ship-like museum building, designed by Danish architect Søren Lund, could be an exhibit in itself. It offers great views of the sand dunes and the sea at Køge Bugt. ⊗ Map B3 • Skovvej 100, Ishøj • 43 54 02 22; Special tours: 43 57 34 55 • Open 10am–5pm Tue–Sun (to 9pm Wed) • Adm; free for under-18s; free with Copenhagen Card • www.arken.dk

6 Karen Blixen Museet

Karen Blixen (pen name: Isak Dinesen), author of the novel *Out of Africa,* was born here in 1885. Blixen returned in 1931 after the death of her lover, Denys Finch Hatton. The house is exactly as it was when she lived here. You can see the furniture she brought back from Nairobi, including Hatton's favourite chair. The museum holds exhibitions of her paintings and drawings, letters, a slide show of her life in Africa and readings by Blixen herself. You can also visit her grave at the foot of Ewald's Hill. ⊗ Map B2 • Rungsted Strandvej 111, Rungsted Kyst • 45 57 10 57 • Open May–Sep: 10am–5pm Tue-Sun; Oct–Apr: 1–4pm Wed–Fri, 11am–4pm Sat–Sun • Adm; free for under-14s; free with Copenhagen Card • Book ahead for guided tours in English • www.blixen.dk

7 Ordrupgaard

This gallery houses a superb collection of French Impressionist art and works by 19th- and 20th-century Danish artists. The building is a 19th-century mansion with a modern extension by architect Zaha Hadid. Within the same complex is furniture designer Finn Juhl's house, now a gallery exhibiting his work. ⊗ Map B2 • Vilvordevej 110, Charlottenlund • 39 64 11 83 • Gallery: open 1–5pm Tue–Fri (to 9pm Wed for special exhibitions only) • Finn Juhl's House: open 11am–4:45pm Sat–Sun & public holidays • Adm; free for under-18s; free with Copenhagen Card • Free audio guide • Book ahead for guided tours in English • www.ordrupgaard.dk

8 Frederiksborg Slot

This copper-turreted, fairy-tale castle stands next to a lake and is surrounded by Baroque gardens. It was built in 1602–20 for Christian IV and replaces an earlier castle built on the site for Frederik II. The interior is a mix of Renaissance and Rococo decor.

Karen Blixen Museet

Den Blå Planet

After a fire in 1859, the castle was rescued from ruin by J C Jacobsen (of Carlsberg fame), who founded a national history museum here. ⊗ *Map B2 • DK-3400 Hillerød • 48 26 04 39 • Museum: open Apr–Oct: 10am–5pm; Nov–Mar: 11am–3pm • Baroque Gardens: 10am–sundown daily • Adm (museum only) • www.dnm.dk*

Charlottenlund Slotshave

The park around Charlottenlund Palace is a 16-minute train ride from the city centre. Redesigned in the Romantic English style in the 19th century, the park's attractions include a charming thatched cottage, once lodgings for the Royal Life Guards. The French chateau-style palace is closed to the public. ⊗ *Map B2 • Open daily • www.slke.dk*

Den Blå Planet

Denmark's national aquarium has garnered much attention for its architecture, a spiralling vortex inspired by the currents of a whirlpool. Inside, there are no less than 53 aquariums in different habitats and over 20,000 marine animals. ⊗ *Map B3 • Jacob Fortlingsvej 1, Kastrup • 44 22 22 44 • Open 10am–6pm daily (until 9pm Mon) • Adm; free with Copenhagen Card • Dis access • www.denblaaplanet.dk*

Day Tour

Morning

Start your day by hopping onto a train at Hovedbanegården and heading to **Helsingør**. Visit **Kronborg Slot** in Helsingør before lunch, and then stop at the **Maritime Museum of Denmark** (see p102). Alternatively, get off the train at **Humlebæk** and visit the **Louisiana Museum** (see p97). If at Helsingør, have an open sandwich and a beer at one of the many pubs at the town square; if in Louisiana, have lunch at the museum restaurant.

Afternoon

After lunch, if you are in Helsingør, wander through the medieval streets, especially **Strandgade** and **Stengade** (see p102). Visit the medieval **Domkirke**, and the **Bymuseum** (see p102), housed in a Carmelite monastery dating back to 1516. If in Louisiana, return to the station and take a train to Rungsted Kyst and drop in at the **Karen Blixen Museet**; try one of the home-made cakes at the café. Or get off the train at Klampenborg to see the fascinating Impressionist paintings at **Ordrupgaard.** If you are in Helsingør or the Karen Blixen Museet, start heading back towards Copenhagen in the early evening, stopping at Klampenborg for an evening of entertainment at the **Bakken Fun Fair**. You can also catch a bite to eat here. If you are at Ordrupgaard, visit the café and then walk to the fun fair; either cut through the park or use the main road. On weekdays, you can wander around the Louisiana Museum till 10pm.

Left **Vikingeskibsmuseet** Centre **Roskilde Kloster** Right **Hestetorvet**

Roskilde

Roskilde Domkirke
This magnificent cathedral holds the remains of 39 Danish monarchs. Map P6 • Domkirkestræde 10 • 46 35 16 24 • Open Apr–Sep: 9am–5pm Mon–Sat, 12:30–5pm Sun; Oct–Mar: 10am–4pm Tue–Sat, 12:30–4pm Sun • Adm; free for under-7s and with Copenhagen Card • www.roskildedomkirke.dk

Stændertorvet
This small square in front of the Town Hall has been a market place since the Middle Ages. Map P6 • Markets on Wed & Sat

Roskilde Palace
Built in 1733–6 for royal visitors, this yellow, four-wing Baroque building houses the Museum of Contemporary Art. Map P6 • Stændertorvet 3 • 46 31 65 70 • Open noon–4pm Tue–Sun • Adm for adults • www.samtidskunst.dk

Roskilde Museum
This museum illustrates Roskilde's history from the time when it was Denmark's first capital. Map P5 • Sankt Ols Gade 15–18 • 46 31 65 29 • Open 11am–4pm daily • Adm for adults; free with Copenhagen Card • www.roskildemuseum.dk

Roskilde Kloster
This manor was bought in 1699 by two aristocratic women who converted it into a home for unmarried mothers. Map P6 • Sankt Peders Straede 8E • 46 35 02 19 • www.roskildekloster.dk

Kirkegård
Now a park, this medieval churchyard holds the graves of many prominent Roskilde citizens. Map Q6

Hestetorvet
The Horse Market is set in what was Roskilde's largest square for centuries. Three giant vases commemorate Roskilde's millennium in 1998. Map Q6

Vikingeskibsmuseet
The popular Viking Ship Museum displays five 1,000-year-old Viking vessels that were recovered from the watery depths in 1962: a warship, longship, ferry and deep sea vessel. Viking-ship boat trips are available May–Sep. Map P4 • Vindeboder 12 • 46 30 02 00 • Open 10am–4pm daily (to 5pm Jul–Aug) • Adm for adults; free for under-18s • www.vikingeskibsmuseet.dk

Musicon
This council-run, former concrete factory is a buzz of creativity, with a dance theatre, skate park, interactive playground and artists' studios. It also hosts regular events and markets. In 2015, Musicon will become home to Denmark's national Museum of Rock Music. Rabalderstræde 1 • 46 31 68 68 • www.musicon.dk

Skomagergade & Algade
The city's two main, beautifully paved streets are lined with shops and cafés. Map P6

Roskilde is home to one of the largest open-air music festivals in Europe, usually the first week in July (www.roskilde-festival.dk).

Left **Femme qui Marche (1932–34), Giacometti** Right **Two Piece Reclining Figure No. 5 (1963–64)**

🔟 Louisiana Museum

Big Thumb (1968)
This striking, 2-m- (6-ft-) tall bronze thumb is modelled after the thumb of its creator, French sculptor César Baldaccini (1921–98).

Dead Drunk Danes (1960)
Rebel artist Asger Jorn (1914–73) was awarded the Guggenheim International Award for this expressive abstract painting. However, he rejected the accolade and sent Harry Guggenheim an infuriated telegram: "Go to hell with your money bastard *stop* Never asked for it *stop* Against all decency to mix artist against his will in your publicity *stop*".

A Closer Grand Canyon (1998)
This monumental, colourful work by David Hockney (1937–) is a series of smaller canvases pieced together to create a vast, landscape-scale vision.

Close Cover Before Striking (1962)
An early Warhol acrylic painting in the Pop Art style. Here, the image of a matchbook is enlarged to the point of abstraction.

Déjeuner sur l'Herbe (1961)
Painted by Pablo Picasso (1881–1973), this abstract work pays homage to Edouard Manet's revolutionary painting of 1862–3, in which a nude woman sits in a classical setting, having a picnic with two clothed modern men.

Alberto Giacometti Collection
The museum owns an impressive collection of 13 sculptures and several drawings by Alberto Giacometti (1901–66). The elongated figures with rough textures are reminiscent of African sculpture.

Two Piece Reclining Figure No 5 (1963–4)
This bronze work by Henry Moore (1898–1986) occupies a beautiful spot between the trees, its humanoid, organic forms melding with the landscape.

Homage to the Yellow Square: Climate (1962)
This is part of the series titled *Homage to the Square* by Josef Albers (1888–1976), the influential Bauhaus artist who explored the chromatic relationship of different coloured flat squares.

Figures in a Landscape (1977)
In this painting by Roy Lichtenstein (1923–97), an exponent of Pop Art, symbols and images are broken down in a Cubist style and set in a surreal landscape.

The Sculpture Park
In the museum's sculpture park, the visual arts, architecture and landscapes exist in unity; the sculptures create silhouettes against the sky, and the gardens enhance the sculptures' appeal. The views are as much a part of the park's charm as its exhibits.

Left **Maritime Museum of Denmark** Right **Axeltorv**

Helsingør

1 Kronborg Slot
Famous as the setting of Shakespeare's *Hamlet*, this castle was built in 1420. Its Great Hall is the largest in Europe. Ⓢ *Map Q2 • Kronborg 2C • 49 21 30 78 • Open Apr–May & Sep–Oct: 11am–4pm daily (closed Mon Nov–Mar); Jun–Aug: 10am–5:30pm daily • Adm; free with Copenhagen Card • www.kronborg.dk*

2 Maritime Museum of Denmark
This interactive museum details Denmark's rich maritime history with hands-on, digital exhibits. Ⓢ *Map Q2 • Ny Kronborgvej 1 • 49 21 06 85 • Open Sep–Jun: 11am–5pm Tue–Sun; Jul–Aug: 10am–5pm daily • Adm; free with Copenhagen Card & for under-18s • Dis access • www.mfs.dk*

3 Festivals
Helsingør's summer festivals include the Maritime Festival Baltic Sail, Sunset Jazz Festival in Hornbæk, and the Hamlet Festival every August at Kronborg. Ⓢ *www.visitnordsjaelland.com*

4 Karmeliterklosteret
This 15th-century Gothic-style monastery belonged to the Carmelite Order. Ⓢ *Map P2 • Sankt Anna Gade 38 • 49 21 17 74 • Church open Tue–Sun 10am–2pm • Book tours for monastery • Adm • www.sctmariae.dk*

5 Helsingør Bymuseum
The Town Museum was once a hospital for sailors. Exhibits here recall its history and more about this medieval town. Ⓢ *Map P2 • Sankt Anna Gade 36 • 49 28 18 00 • Open noon–4pm Tue–Fri & Sun, 10am–2pm Sat • Adm; free with Copenhagen Card*

6 Axeltorv
This main square features a statue of Erik of Pomerania, the Polish prince who ruled Denmark from 1397 to 1439. Ⓢ *Map P2*

7 Stengade & Strandgade
Stengade is a pedestrianized street in the medieval quarter. Some houses on Strandgade date back to the 1400s; No 91 is now the Museet Skibsklarerergaarden. Ⓢ *Map P3 • www.skibsklarerergaarden.dk*

8 Sankt Olai Kirke (Helsingør Domkirke)
Note the 15th-century crucifix, the 1568 Renaissance pulpit, the 1579 baptismal font and the carved wooden altar. Ⓢ *Map P2 • Sankt Anna Gade 12 • 49 21 04 43 • Open May–Aug: 10am–4pm Mon–Fri (to 2pm Sep–Apr) • www.helsingoerdomkirke.dk*

9 Danmarks Teknisk Museum
The collection of machines here includes steam engines, cars and aeroplanes. Ⓢ *Fabriksvej 25 • 49 22 26 11 • Open 10am–5pm Tue–Sun • Adm for adults • www.tekniskmuseum.dk*

10 Øresundsakvariet
This aquarium has a variety of tropical fish and Baltic species. Ⓢ *Map P1 • Strandpromenaden 5 • 35 32 19 70 • Open Jun–Aug: 10am–5pm daily; Sep–May: 10am–4pm Mon–Fri, 10am–5pm Sat–Sun • Adm; free with Copenhagen Card*

Price Categories

For a three-course meal for one without alcohol, including taxes and extra charges.	⊛ up to 200 Dkr
	⊛⊛ 200–300
	⊛⊛⊛ 300–400
	⊛⊛⊛⊛ 400–500
	⊛⊛⊛⊛⊛ over 500 Dkr

Søstrene Olsen

Places to Eat

Café Bomhuset

1 An upscale alternative to the typical outdoor café with food to match. The large terrace is popular. ✎ Map B2 • Skovriderkroen, Strandvejen 235, Charlottenlund • 39 65 67 00 • Open daily • www.cafebomhuset.dk • ⊛⊛⊛

Restaurant Sletten

2 Sharing its owners with Formel B (see p49), Sletten serves French cuisine at lower prices, with the bonus of a sea view. ✎ Map B2 • Gl. Strandvej 137, Humlebæk • 49 19 13 21 • Closed Sun–Mon Sep–May • www.sletten.dk • ⊛⊛⊛⊛

Café Jorden Rundt

3 This unusual café offers great sea views from its curved, panoramic windows. Popular for brunch, soups, sandwiches and cakes. ✎ Map B2 • Strandvejen 152, Charlottenlund • 39 63 73 81 • ⊛⊛

Den Gule Cottage

4 This timber-framed restaurant was created in 1844 by architect Bindesbøll. Dishes are prepared with seasonal ingredients. ✎ Map B2 • Strandvejen 506, Klampenborg • 39 64 06 91 • Closed Mon–Wed mid-Nov–Dec & mid-Feb–May; mid-Dec–mid-Feb • www.dengulecottage.dk • ⊛⊛⊛⊛⊛

Mumm

5 On one of Roskilde's oldest streets, this tiny French-Danish restaurant has a pretty summer courtyard. ✎ Map N6 • Karen Oldsdatters Stræde 9, Roskilde • 46 37 22 01 • Dinner only; closed Sun • ⊛⊛⊛⊛

Restaurant Gilleleje Havn

6 Enjoy traditional Danish seafood at this old seamen's inn (1895) on the harbour. After the meal, stroll along the sandy beach. ✎ Map A1 • Havnevej 14, Gilleleje • 48 30 30 39 • Open Wed–Sun; closed lunch Wed • www.gillelejehavn.dk • ⊛⊛⊛

Søllerød Kro

7 One of Denmark's finest, this Michelin-starred restaurant offers both set menus and à la carte dishes, all impeccably presented. ✎ Map B2 • Søllerødveg 35, Holte • 45 80 25 05 • Closed Mon–Tue • www.soellered-kro.dk • ⊛⊛⊛⊛⊛

Den Røde Cottage

8 Neighbouring Den Gule Cottage, Den Røde has a Michelin star for its fresh, seasonal menus. ✎ Map B2 • Strandvejen 550, Klampenborg • 39 90 46 14 • Dinner only; closed Feb, Oct–Apr Sun • www.denroedecottage.dk • ⊛⊛⊛⊛⊛

Snekken

9 Next door to the Vikingeskibsmuseet (see p100), Snekken offers sea views and contemporary Nordic cuisine using many ingredients from Viking times. ✎ Map P4 • Vindeboder 16, Roskilde • 46 35 98 16 • www.snekken.dk • ⊛⊛⊛⊛

Søstrene Olsen

10 The food at this cottage-style restaurant is delicious. The seafood is particularly good. ✎ Map B1 • Øresundsvej 10, Hornbæk • 49 70 05 50 • Closed Tue–Wed • www.sostreneolsen.dk • ⊛⊛⊛

STREETSMART

Getting There
and Around
106

General Information
107

Health and Security
108

Banking and
Communications
109

Things To Avoid
110

Copenhagen on
a Budget
111

Luxury Hotels
112

Expensive Hotels
113

Mid-Range Hotels
114

Budget Hotels
115

Other Accommodation
116

Rooms with a View
117

COPENHAGEN'S TOP 10

Left **SAS plane** Right **International ferry**

Getting There and Around

1 Arriving by Air

Airlines that serve Copenhagen directly are Scandinavian Airlines (SAS), British Airways, easyJet and Norwegian. The airport is 12 km (7 miles) away from the city; it takes about 15 mins to get to the city by train or Metro, or 45 mins by bus (both cost the same). You will also find a taxi rank just outside the airport (terminal 3).

2 Arriving by Train

International trains run to and from many European cities, including Hamburg and Berlin. All international trains stop at Hovedbanegården, the city's main station.

3 Arriving by Road

If driving into Copenhagen from Sweden, you can take the Øresund bridge from Malmø. If driving in from Germany and crossing the island of Funen, you can take the Great Belt Bridge to Sjælland, the island on which the city is built. Both bridges exact a toll.

4 Arriving by Ferry

You can take a Polferries ferry from Poland (Swinoujscie) or a DFDS Seaways ferry from Norway (Oslo). Ferries from the UK (Harwich) stop at Esbjerg; from here, you can take a train to Copenhagen or drive 300 km (186 miles) on the E20 motorway.

5 Local Public Transport

The bus, local (S) train and Metro systems are frequent and efficient. In Greater Copenhagen, you can use a single ticket or buy a smartcard, a pre-pay card which can be topped up and used on all three systems. Smartcards work out cheaper than buying individual tickets. ✪ www.dsb.dk

6 Harbour Buses

Harbour buses (991, 992, 993) run the length of the harbour between Nordre Toldbod (near Gefionspringvandet), past Den Sorte Diamant to Teglholmen, south of Fisketorvet. ✪ Daily 7am–7pm Mon–Fri, from 10am Sat–Sun, approx. every 15 minutes at peak time, hourly at other times

7 Taxis & Rickshaws

Taxis have a FRI (free) sign on the roof. You can pay by credit card and also get receipts. Catch the cycle rickshaws for short rides from Storkespringvandet, Tivoli, Rådhuspladsen and Nyhavn.

8 Driving & Parking

You can drive if you are over 18 and hold a valid licence. Always carry the registration papers and a reflecting triangle. Parkering forbudt means no parking within certain time limits. Motoring offences attract on-the-spot fines.

9 Bicycles

Bicycles offer a great way to enjoy Copenhagen. There are cycle paths throughout the city. Free city bikes are available from mid-April to mid-December at 110 stands around the city.

10 On Foot

Copenhagen is a lovely place to walk around. Many of the sights are a short walk away from each other, unless you plan on heading out to Nørrebro or crossing town. Tourist signposting is helpful.

Directory

Copenhagen Airport
• 32 31 32 31
• www.cph.dk

DSB Train Tickets Reservation and Info
• 70 13 14 15
• www.dsb.dk

Ferries
• DFDS Seaways: 78 79 24 74; www.dfdsseaways.dk
• Polferries (Swinoujscie): 44 45 12 80; www.polferries.com/ferry

Car Hire
• Budget Rent A Car: 33 55 05 00
• Europcar: 70 11 33 55; www.europcar.dk

Bicycle Information
• Københavns Cykelbør: www.cykelborsen.dk
• Baisikeli Bike Rental: www.baisikeli.dk

Preceding pages: **Pusher Street in Christiania, Christianshavn.**

Left **Airport information board** Centre **Tourist information sign** Right **Copenhagen Visitors Centre**

General Information

Best Time to Visit
Summertime is ideal since you can enjoy as many as 16–18 hours of daylight on clear days. Christmas is also fun, with fairy lights and celebrations at Tivoli, the open-air ice rinks and plenty of markets, concerts and other entertainment. There is plenty for kids to do on other Danish school holidays as well: week 7, July to mid-August, and week 42. The only time you might want to avoid, due to chilly winds and the limited hours of daylight (just 7), is Dec–Jan.

Visas
European Union citizens do not require a visa to enter Denmark and can stay for up to 90 days. Others should check whether their country has reciprocal agreements on waiving visa requirements. Foreign nationals who wish to work in Copenhagen must have a work and residence permit for paid or unpaid work. ◈ www.nyidanmark.dk/en-us/coming_to_dk/

Duty Free Goods & Customs
Denmark imposes a limit on what can be brought into the country. Do not carry food articles that are not vacuum-packed by the manufacturer. Articles in commercial quantities and presents valued at more than 1,350 Dkr are subject to customs duty. US citizens are liable to pay duty if carrying goods worth more than $400. Many shops offer tax-free shopping for non-EU visitors for a minimum purchase of 300 Dkr; remember to collect a Global Refund Tax Free Cheque from the store, so you can apply for a 13–19 per cent refund. ◈ www.global-blue.com

Tourist Information
The Copenhagen Visitors Centre is located close to the main station. It offers a wealth of information, as well as hotel bookings, car rental, the Copenhagen Card (see p111) and information about tours. ◈ Map G5
• Copenhagen Visitors Centre, Vesterbrogade 4A
• 70 22 24 42 • www.visitcopenhagen.com

Opening Hours
Opening hours for shops are: Mon–Thu 9:30am/10am–5:30pm; Fri 9:30am/10am–7pm/8pm; Sat 9:30am/10am–3pm (to 5pm on the first Saturday of the month). Since the trading laws have been relaxed, larger shops now open on Sundays. Weekend hours may be extended in tourist areas, especially in summer. Most museums are closed on Mondays.

Weekly Listings
The Copenhagen Post (each Friday) lists events taking place in the city. Danish-speakers can check the Friday guide sections of Politiken and Berlingske.

Websites
Tourist board websites provide useful information. Other websites are listed below. ◈ www.visitcopenhagen.com
• www.visitdenmark.com
• www.aok.dk/english
• www.cph-tourist.dk

Public Holidays
Public holidays include New Year's Day, Maundy Thursday, Good Friday, Easter Monday, Common Prayer Day, Ascension Day, Whit Monday and Christmas.

Admission Prices
Some museums are always free, others are mostly free on Wednesdays. The Copenhagen Card offers discounts and allows entry to 72 attractions and museums.

For Children
Several museums have children's facilities. Most restaurants provide high chairs and offer children's menus. Some hotels provide play areas and activity packages for children, while others offer baby-sitting services. The airport has play areas, baby-changing facilities and buggies.

Left **Pharmacy sign** Right **Police van**

Health and Security

1 Health Insurance & Precautions

Although emergency medical treatment is free, make sure you have suitable travel insurance. EU nationals should bring their European Health Insurance cards. Visitors from Schengen countries (several EU countries plus Iceland, Norway and Switzerland) can carry up to 30 days' supply of prescribed medication; others must carry no more than 14 days' supply. Documents stating the need for the medication may be required.

2 Pharmacies

Pharmacies have a green sign saying "A" (*Apotek*). Prescription medication can only be bought at pharmacies. Credit cards are not accepted; full payment is required. ◈ *Steno Apotek, Vesterbrogade 6C (opposite main station)*

3 Medical Treatment

Tourists are covered by public health services as per the agreement between Denmark and their home country. Emergency hospital treatment is free for all tourists, unless the medical facility determines that the emergency occurred as a result of a pre-existing condition. Refunds for doctor's fees can be obtained from the nearest municipal or health insurance office before leaving Denmark.

4 Personal Safety

Copenhagen is a safe city, but visitors must take precautions. Make sure your bags are closed securely and your credit cards, mobile and money are kept in a safe place. If you are a victim of a crime, contact the police immediately *(see below)*.

5 Police

To file reports, contact the nearest police station *(see Directory)*. In a crisis, call the emergency services number.

6 Dental Treatment

Head to Dentist Tandlægevagten (Oslo Plads 14, tel. 70 25 00 41), open 8am–9:30pm Mon–Fri, 10am–noon Sat–Sun. Be prepared to pay at least 150 Dkr on the spot. For emergency treatment call 1813.

7 Doctors & Hospitals

Outside office hours, call Doctor On Call. If an emergency arises, go to the Accident and Emergency section of any hospital *(see Directory)*.

8 Theft

Report theft at a police station immediately; you will be issued with a crime report note, which you will need for any insurance claims.

9 Disabled Access

The Copenhagen Visitors Centre *(see p107)* has a list of places that offer facilities for the disabled. You can also contact DSB Handicap *(see Directory)*.

10 Lost Property

For items lost on the bus, call 36 13 14 15; for items lost on local (S)-train: 70 13 14 15. Lost property office: 38 74 88 22.

(see p107)

Directory

24-hour Pharmacy
• Steno Apotek: 33 14 82 66

Police
• Station City: Halmtorvet 20; 33 14 14 48
• Slotsherrensvej (lost and found): 38 74 88 22
• 114 (for non-emergencies)

Emergency Services
• Ambulance, Fire & Police: 112

Doctors & Hospitals
• Doctor On Call: 1813
• Amager Hospital: 32 34 32 34
• Bispebjerg Hospital: 35 31 35 31
• Frederiksberg Hospital: 38 16 38 16
• Hvidovre Hospital: 38 62 38 62

Handicap Services
• DSB Handicap Service: 70 13 14 15 and then press 6
• 4 x 35 Taxi (book ahead): 35 35 35 35
• Accessibility Label Scheme: www.godadgang.dk

Left **Using Wi-Fi by the canal** Centre **ATM machine** Right **Danish postbox**

🔟 Banking and Communications

1 Local Currency
Danish notes come in denominations of 1,000 Dkr, 500 Dkr, 200 Dkr, 100 Dkr and 50 Dkr. Coins come in 20 Dkr, 10 Dkr, 5 Dkr, 2 Dkr, 1 Dkr and 50 øre (half a krone).

2 Banks & ATMs
Banks are usually open Mon–Wed 10am–10pm, Thu 10am–6pm. Most ATMs are open 24 hours a day, and are usually found outside banks and Metro stations. The most popular debit and credit card is Visa, but finding machines that accept MasterCard or American Express shouldn't be a problem, either.

3 Exchange
There are many exchange bureaux across the city. Those open for longest include the Danske Bank exchange office (6am–10pm) at Copenhagen Airport, and the Forex (8am–9pm) at Hovedbånegard station. Hotels have foreign exchange services, but the rate is substantially lower than at banks or exchange bureaux.

4 Credit Cards
International credit cards are not always accepted, especially at small outlets. There may also be an extra charge if you pay by credit card. If you lose your credit card, call your credit card company immediately (see Directory).

5 Post Offices
Post offices are usually open Mon–Fri 9am/10am–5.30pm, Sat 9am–noon (or closed). You can arrange for a Poste Restante service at any post office. International mail arrives faster with the Faste Deliver A-mail or Prioritaire mail service.
🌐 www.postdanmark.dk

6 Telephones
The international dialling code for Denmark is +45; there are no area codes. To make international calls from Denmark, first dial 00. Public telephones accept coins and pre-paid phone cards. Insert 5–20 Dkr for international calls; however, you will not receive change. You cannot make collect calls to the US from public phones. For information and directory assistance, call 113.

7 Mobiles
GSM compatible mobile phones will work. There are three main service providers (see Directory). Roaming is expensive, so check your service provider's rates for calls from abroad.

8 Internet
Most hotels offer Internet access, many with Wi-Fi in rooms. Free Wi-Fi is also available on many buses and trains, as well as in some cafés and public spaces.

9 TV & Radio
Cable and satellite TV provide access to channels in English and other languages. Although DR Radio has stopped broadcasting current affairs in English, it does update its website with the news in English.

10 Newspapers & Magazines
Denmark's national newspapers include: *Borsen*, *Ekstra Bladet*, *Jyllands-Posten*, *Information* and *Politiken*. For local news in English, get the *Copenhagen Post* (25 Dkr). You can find most major UK and US newspapers at city centre kiosks.

Directory

Credit Card Companies
• AMEX:
70 20 70 97
• MasterCard:
80 01 60 98
• Visa and other cards:
44 89 29 29
• Danish "Nets" 24-hr hotline (for other credit cards):
44 89 27 50
• Diners Club:
36 73 73 73

Mobile Companies
• TDC-Mobil:
70 70 30 30
• Telenor:
72 10 01 00
• Telia:
80 40 40 29

Left **Traffic lights at a pedestrian crossing** Right **People waiting to cross a street**

🔟 Things to Avoid

Jaywalking
The Danes hardly ever jaywalk, even if there is no traffic in either direction. If you can't resist the urge to do so, don't be surprised if a grumpy policeman decides to arrest you for breaking the law. Always cross at a pedestrian crossing when the signal turns green. For the benefit of the visually impaired, a beeping sound is emitted for the entire duration when it is safe to cross.

Exceeding the Speed Limit or Drinking & Driving
Exceeding the speed limit is illegal and you can be fined on the spot. If you don't pay, your car may be impounded. Drinking and driving is strictly prohibited as well. Do not drive if the level of alcohol content in your blood is more than 0.5 (two drinks). For alcohol levels of up to 1.2, a large fine is imposed. If the level is 1.2–2, you could lose your licence. Levels above 2 may result in a prison sentence of two weeks or more.

Buying Drugs
Buying and selling drugs in Denmark is illegal, just as in most other places, and the penalties are severe. Once, buying drugs from a booth on Pusher Street in Christiania was almost *de rigueur* for young visitors. However, Pusher Street has now been shut down and drugs cannot be bought openly.

Forgetting to Clip Tickets on Public Transport
Always remember to clip your ticket to validate it when you travel on public transport. Clipping machines can be found on buses and on platforms of train and Metro stations. If you do not clip your ticket, you can be fined by inspectors.

Visiting Museums on Monday Without Checking
Most museums are shut on Mondays, though a few are closed on Tuesdays instead. So check in advance for frustration-free sightseeing.

Stepping Out in Front of a Bike
Visitors who are not used to having cycle lanes in their cities might mistake this area for part of the pavement. However, bikes have right of way here. Remember to treat cycle lanes as you would the rest of the road.

Grumbling in English
Practically everyone below the age of 70 (and many above) speaks excellent English, as they have been watching English and American films and TV for a long time. So, if you grumble in English, everyone will know exactly what you are saying.

Praising the Swedes
The Danes and their neighbours, the Swedes, have been at loggerheads for centuries. These days, the Danes continue to be rude about the Swedes, but in a tongue-in-cheek way. However, they often do mean it when they say that the Swedes travel to Copenhagen only to buy alcohol, as it is less expensive here.

Insulting the Royal Family
The Danes are very respectful of their royal family, especially the present queen. Insulting them is highly inadvisable; it would be similar to (if not a little worse) insulting someone's favourite sports team. However unintentional it may be, it could damage your relations with your hosts – especially the older generation.

Not Making Eye Contact When "Skolling" a Drink
It is considered rude if you don't lock your gaze with your drinking partner when you raise a toast and say "*Skål*". This tradition of "skolling" dates back to the Vikings, who used to chop off the heads of vanquished enemy chiefs and drink out of their skulls.

Left **Café in Vesterbro** Right **Gardens of the Royal Library**

10 Copenhagen on a Budget

1 Reservations
Make your hotel reservations well in advance to get the best deals. The peak season is usually Apr/May–Sept/Oct. Online hotel prices are often cheaper and many hotels have lower rates at weekends, but it is a good idea to ring the hotel and ask about their best prices and deals.

2 Sights
A well-planned trip can be surprisingly inexpensive. Walking the streets is free and also fascinating. Discount smartcards *(see p106)* reduce your expense on public transport. Parks and gardens (except Tivoli) are free, and often host free entertainment, especially in the summer. Several state-run museums are free; others are free on Wednesdays or Sundays. The Danish National Theatre sells unsold tickets at half price after 4pm on the day of the performance. ✆ *Danish National Theatre box office: Tordenskjoldsgade 7*

3 The Copenhagen Card
The Copenhagen Card is a good investment, offering lots of great discounts for sightseeing and transport. For information, or to buy the Copenhagen Card in advance (minimum of 10 days), visit the Copenhagen Visitors' Centre website *(see p107)*.

4 Cheap Eats
As in most other places, pizza and pasta dishes are cheap in Copenhagen. Fast-food outlets are plentiful, and you can get a sandwich or a burger and chips for around 50 Dkr. If you want something more substantial for under 150 Dkr, a main course, bread and a glass of wine or beer in a café will easily fit your budget. Some restaurants, especially Thai, offer great value buffet lunches.

5 Hotel Breakfasts
Although breakfast is a modest affair for most Danes, visitors are spoiled for choice at hotels. Eat-all-you-want breakfasts offer good value for money, even at 100–150 Dkr – especially if you can fill up for the day. Some hotels include breakfast in the price of the room, so check when you book.

6 Meals
Lunch *(Frokost)* is served from noon to 2pm. Dinner *(Aftensmad)* is usually served from 6pm to 9:30pm/10pm, although you can call to check if the kitchen is open after that. Dinner often costs more, but you are served larger portions. Late-night snacks are limited to hot dogs or kebabs from a stall.

7 Tipping
Tips are usually included in bills at restaurants and hotels, so it is not considered rude if you don't leave one. In cheaper places, rounding the bill up is perfectly acceptable. In more expensive restaurants, it is customary to leave a tip, but it can be as little as 5 per cent of the bill. You don't have to tip taxi drivers.

8 Free Music Events
Every Wednesday in the spring and summer, students from the Royal Danish Academy of Music perform classical concerts at the Teatermuseet. Look out for the street bands at the jazz festival in July *(see p43)* and for Friday Rock at Tivoli *(see p11)*. ✆ *www.onsdagskoncerter. dk • www.jazzfestival.dk*

9 Other Free Events
During Christmas, special markets are held, with some shops like the Royal Copenhagen *(see p68)* putting on exhibitions. Free skating is on offer at rinks at Toftegård Plads in Valby, Frederiksberg Runddel and Blågårds Plads. Museums conduct free workshops for kids (closed 24–25 Dec).

10 Movies
Some cinemas offer lower rates from Mon to Thu before 6pm (ring to check). In Jul–Aug, free open-air screenings are held by Zulu Sommerbio. ✆ *www.zulu.dk*

Discover more at www.dk.com

Left **Hotel Alexandra** Right **Palace Hotel**

Luxury Hotels

Palace Hotel
This Victorian hotel overlooks Rådhuspladsen and combines traditional English decor with a modern twist. The hotel was used in the Copenhagen episode of *Midsomer Murders*. The bar is popular with locals. ✆ *Map H5 • Rådhuspladsen 57 • 33 14 40 50 • www. palacehotelcopenhagen.com • ®®®®*

Hotel d'Angleterre
Established in 1755, olden-day grandeur meets modern luxury at this hotel. It has a plush palm court, banquet rooms, a spa and an elegant restaurant serving international cuisine. ✆ *Map K4 • Kongens Nytorv 34 • 33 12 00 95 • www. dangleterre.dk • ®®®®®*

Hotel Alexandra
More than a century old, this excellent hotel is popular for its original, 20th-century furniture, with design classics ranging from Kaare Klint chairs to Akademi chandeliers designed by Poul Henningsen. There are three non-smoking floors as well as allergy-tested rooms. ✆ *Map G5 • H C Andersens Boulevard 8 • 33 74 44 44 • www. hotelalexandra.dk • ®®®®*

Hotel Front
This modern, child-friendly boutique hotel offers rooms of various sizes. Each has been individually decorated

and enhanced with attractive artwork. ✆ *Map L4 • Skt Annæ Plads 21 • 33 13 34 00 • www. scandichotels.dk/front • ®®®®*

Sankt Petri
Every room of this five-star hotel is delightfully decorated with orchids and abstract art, and the bathrooms are luxurious. It has a lively glass-roofed atrium featuring international DJs, as well as a popular cocktail bar. ✆ *Map H4 • Krystalgade 22 • 33 45 91 00 • www.sktpetri.com • ®®®®®*

Nimb Hotel
Copenhagen's most exclusive hotel has just 17 rooms. Each one is unique and luxurious, and features range from open fireplaces to flatscreen TVs. Housed in the landmark Nimb building and with its own limousine service, this is A-list accommodation. ✆ *Map G5 • Bernstorffs-gade 5 • 88 70 00 00 • www.nimb.dk • ®®®®®*

Nyhavn 71
This charming four-star hotel at the end of Nyhavn was once a warehouse built to store goods from ships in the harbour. The area is very peaceful and does not suffer from noisy tourists; few wander this far down the quayside. The restaurant offers a substantial breakfast.

✆ *Map L4 • Nyhavn 71 • 33 43 62 00 • www. 71nyhavnhotel.com • ®®®®*

Copenhagen Plaza
Built in 1913, this historic hotel has spacious rooms and traditional decor. The Library Bar, full of 18th-century books, is one of the best bars in the city. ✆ *Map G5 • Bernstorffsgade 4 • 33 14 92 62 • www.profilhotels. com/copenhagenplaza • ®®®®*

Hilton Copen-hagen Airport
This is a swanky five-star hotel, equipped with a spa, pool, gym, three restaurants and bars and good business facilities. The decor is distinctly Scandinavian with plenty of light wood. ✆ *Ellehammersvej, 20 Kastrup • 32 50 15 01 • www.hiltonnordics.com • ®®®®®*

Radisson Blu Scandinavia
With 544 rooms, this is one of the largest hotels in Copenhagen, offering great views of Christianshavn and the city. Its world-class facilities include Copenhagen's only casino and four restaurants – check out the 25th-floor Dining Room, with panoramic views across the Øresund. ✆ *Map J6 • Amager Boulevard 70 • 33 96 50 00 • www. radissonblu.com • ®®®®*

Avenue Hotel

Price Categories

For a standard,
double room per
night (with breakfast
if included), taxes
and extra charges.

⊛	up to 700 Dkr
⊛⊛	700–1,000
⊛⊛⊛	1,000–1,200
⊛⊛⊛⊛	1,200–1,600
⊛⊛⊛⊛⊛	over 1,600 Dkr

🔟 Expensive Hotels

1 Hotel Twentyseven

This boutique hotel, with its minimalist decor, is centrally located not far from Strøget and Rådhuspladsen. The trendy bars include a wine bar, cocktail lounge and the Icebar Copenhagen. ⊛ Map H5 • Løngangstræde 27 • 70 27 56 27 • www.hotel27.dk • ⊛⊛⊛

2 Phoenix

Owned by the Arp-Hansen group, this four-star hotel, off Kongens Nytorv, is decorated in a French, Louis XIV style with contemporary colour and touch. Housed in a 17th-century building, the hotel has a restaurant and "English pub"-style bar. ⊛ Map L3 • Bredgade 37 • 33 95 95 00 • www.phoenixcopenhagen.com • ⊛⊛⊛⊛

3 Imperial Hotel

Stylish and welcoming, this four-star hotel has been decorated in modern Danish design and has an entire floor dedicated to the work of the Danish designer Børge Mogensen. ⊛ Map G5 • Vester Farmimagsgade 9 • 33 12 80 00 • www.imperial-hotel-copenhagen.com • ⊛⊛⊛

4 Babette Guldsmeden

In a peaceful location close to the green area of Kastellet (see p78), this hotel is housed inside a 19th-century building. Services include free organic coffee and a 24-hour snack bar. ⊛ Map L2 • Bredgade 78 • 33 48 10 00 • www.guldsmeden hotels.com • ⊛⊛⊛⊛

5 Grand Hotel

A short walk down Vesterbrogade, this classic four-star hotel is located close to Tivoli. In summer, its pavement café is ideal for people-watching. The rooms are spacious, and the decor traditional without being ornate. The hotel's Restaurant Frascati is very good and serves Italian cuisine. ⊛ Map G5 • Vesterbrogade 9 • 33 27 69 00 • www.grandhotel. dk • ⊛⊛⊛

6 Hotel SP34

This stylish boutique hotel is located in the Latin Quarter, close to Rådhuspladsen. There are 118 beautifully furnished rooms, all with free Wi-Fi and cable TV. The hotel has two restaurants, a lounge bar, a café and a rooftop terrace. The buffet breakfast is organic. ⊛ Map G4 • Sankt Peders Stræde 34 • 33 13 30 00 • www.brochner-hotels.dk • ⊛⊛⊛⊛

7 Kong Arthur

This four-star hotel is located inside a large courtyard. It exudes old-world charm, and offers large family rooms and a conservatory-style breakfast room. ⊛ Map G3 • Nørre Søgade 11 • 33 45 77 77 • www. arthurhotels.dk • ⊛⊛⊛⊛

8 First Hotel Kong Frederik

There have been inns and hotels on this site since the 14th century, but this hotel dates back to 1868. Extensively renovated, this classic, English-style four-star hotel also offers a secluded courtyard lounge around the back. ⊛ Map H4 • Vester Voldgade 25 • 33 12 59 02 • www.firsthotels.com • ⊛⊛⊛

9 Christian IV

Ideally located away from the busy city centre, this three-star hotel is a stone's throw away from Kongens Have and Rosenborg Slot (see pp14–15). There are a range of great free services on offer, including coffee or tea and snacks served through the day and entry to the gym on Adelsgade. Check for the best prices. ⊛ Map K3 • Dronningens Tværgade 45 • 33 32 10 44 • www. hotelchristianiv.dk • ⊛⊛⊛⊛

10 Avenue Hotel

This independent boutique hotel is located on the edge of Frederiksberg, close to both the Lakes (see p44) and the lively Nørrebro district. A hotel since 1939, it offers child-friendly, spacious family rooms. There is even a sandpit on the terrace, where breakfasts can also be enjoyed. ⊛ Map C4 • Åboulevard 29 • 35 37 31 11 • www.avenuehotel.dk • ⊛⊛⊛⊛

Left **First Hotel Mayfair** Right **The Square**

🔟 Mid-Range Hotels

1 Carlton Hotel Guldsmeden

This hotel is close to the main station. Sophisticated yet relaxed, it has an ethnic decor with dark-wood furniture, whitewashed walls and Egyptian cotton sheets. It offers delicious organic breakfasts. ◆ Map C5 • Vesterbrogade 66 • 33 22 15 00 • www. hotelguldsmeden.dk • ⓚⓚⓚ

2 First Hotel Mayfair

Close to the city's main attractions, this comfortable hotel is furnished mainly in an English style with a hint of the Oriental. ◆ Map G6 • Helgolandsgade 3 • 70 12 17 00 • www.firsthotels. com • ⓚⓚⓚ

3 Savoy

This 66-room hotel, dating from 1906, is known for its distinctive Art Nouveau façade, and is a Vesterbro landmark. Thoroughly renovated but still affordably priced, it has Wi-Fi connection in all rooms and a guest PC in the lobby. Rooms facing the courtyard are much quieter. ◆ Map C5 • Vesterbrogade 34 • 33 26 75 00 • www.savoyhotel. dk • ⓚⓚ

4 Radisson Blu Falconer

Smaller than the other two Radisson hotels in the city, this bright and airy hotel offers a wide range of services

and conveniences. It is primarily aimed at business travellers. ◆ Map B4 • Falkoner Allé 9 • 38 15 80 01 • www. radissonblu.com • ⓚⓚⓚ

5 Opera

This three-star hotel is located under the arches of the Kongelige Teater in a building that dates back to 1869. It has operated as a hotel since the 1950s. The decor is modern with traditional English overtones, such as Regency-striped armchairs. ◆ Map K4 • Tordenskjoldsgade 15 • 33 47 83 00 • www. hotelopera.dk • ⓚⓚ

6 Ibsens Hotel

This urban boutique hotel is located in the Nansensgade area of the city, a short walk from Nørreport station. All rooms are non-smoking and individually decorated and there is a beautiful courtyard. ◆ Map G3 • Vendersgade 23 • 33 13 19 13 • www. arthurhotels.dk/ibsens-hotel/ • ⓚⓚⓚ

7 Axel Hotel Guldsmeden

This boutique hotel is a surprising find close to the main train station. Relax in the saunas and steam baths of the hotel spa and enjoy organic breakfasts in the heated courtyard. ◆ Map G6 • Helgolandsgade 11 • 33 31 32 66 • www. hotelguldsmeden.dk • ⓚⓚⓚ

8 The Square

This modern three-star hotel is located on the Town Hall square. It comes with stylish pony-hair chairs at the entrance and Arne Jacobsen chairs in the reception area. The rooms are comfortable and the breakfast on offer is excellent. ◆ Map H5 • Rådhuspladsen 14 • 33 38 12 00 • www.thesquare. dk • ⓚⓚⓚ

9 Comfort Hotel Vesterbro

This fabulous four-star hotel has a good location on Vesterbrogade. It has large, attractive rooms with minimalist decor. There is a wonderful atrium with potted trees where you can catch a bite to eat. Interestingly, in the seedier days of Vesterbro, it was the local porn cinema. ◆ Map C5 • Vesterbrogade 23–9 • 33 78 80 00 • www. nordicchoicehotels.com • ⓚⓚⓚ

10 Tivoli Hotel

This high-rise hotel opened in 2010. There are indoor and outdoor activities for kids, as well as a swimming pool and fitness centre. Part of the Tivoli Congress Center, it also caters for business guests. A free shuttle bus operates between the hotel and Tivoli. ◆ Map D6 • Arni Magnussons Gade 2 • 44 87 00 00 • www.tivolihotel. com • ⓚⓚⓚ

Price Categories

For a standard, double room per	⑨ up to 700 Dkr
	⑨⑨ 700–1,000
night (with breakfast if included), taxes	⑨⑨⑨ 1,000–1,200
	⑨⑨⑨⑨ 1,200–1,600
and extra charges.	⑨⑨⑨⑨⑨ over 1,600 Dkr

Hotel Copenhagen

🔟 Budget Hotels

1 Generator Hostel Copenhagen

A smart, modern hostel with private, en-suite rooms as well as dorms. Facilities include Wi-Fi, a bar and breakfast (for an extra charge). ◈ *Map K4 • Adelgade 5–7 • 78 77 54 00 • www.generator hostels.com* • ⑨

2 Zleep Hotel Copenhagen City

This 19th-century hotel has reasonably sized en-suite rooms, with TVs and Internet connection. The neighbourhood is central but can be noisy. Breakfast buffet extra. ◈ *Map G6 • Helgolandsgade 14 • 43 68 23 18 • www. zleephotels.com* • ⑨

3 WakeUp Copenhagen Carsten Niebuhrs

Designed by Kim Utzon, this ultra-modern, two-star budget hotel is located along the water-front, close to Fisketorvet shopping centre. Its 510 rooms are spread over 12 floors, with prices rising per floor. ◈ *Map D6 • Carsten Niebuhrs Gade 11 • 44 80 00 10 • www. wakeupcopenhagen.dk* • ⑨⑨

4 Hotel Sct. Thomas

A family-run hotel, Sct. Thomas is located in a quiet residential area, yet close to Vesterbro and Værnedamsvej *(see p86)*. The cosy rooms come with shared or private bathrooms and breakfast is included. ◈ *Map C5 • Frederiksberg Allé 7 • 33 21 64 64 • www. hotelsctthomas.dk* • ⑨⑨

5 Wakeup Copenhagen Borgergade

This 498-room hotel offers ultra-modern accommodation just minutes from Kongens Nytorv, Amalienborg and other city-centre sights. ◈ *Map K3 • Borgergade 9 • 44 80 00 00 • www. wakeupcopenhagen.dk* • ⑨⑨⑨

6 Cab Inn City

Based on the idea of a ship's cabin, the rooms at Cab Inn City are small but perfectly designed, with all the modern conveniences tucked into a clever storage design. You can pick from bunk beds in twin rooms, double rooms and family rooms. The hotel has a pleasant ambience and offers good buffet break-fasts. ◈ *Map H6 • City Mitchellsgade 14 • 33 46 16 16 • Dis access • www. cabinn.com* • ⑨

7 Cab Inn Express

This three-star hotel in the popular chain is just a 12-minute walk from Rådhuspladsen, situated on the other side of the reservoirs. If you walk down the road and look across the water, you will be able to see the Tycho Brahe Planetarium *(see p84)*. ◈ *Map C4 • Danasvej 32, Frederiksberg • 33 21 04 00 • www.cabinn.com* • ⑨

8 Cab Inn Scandinavia

This Cab Inn hotel is located just a block away from the Cab Inn Express and a road before the Peblinge Lake. It is equipped with all the modern conveniences found at the other three Cab Inns in the city. ◈ *Map C4 • Vodroffsvej 55, Frederiksberg • 35 36 11 11 • www.cabinn.com* • ⑨

9 Cab Inn Metro

The Cab Inn Metro is the fourth hotel in the city's budget Cab Inn concept, and is Denmark's largest hotel. It is located close to the airport and Fields shopping centre. All 710 rooms are modern and clean with en-suite facilities. Free wireless Internet access is included in the price. ◈ *Arne Jakobsens Allé 2 • 32 46 57 00 • www. cabinn.com* • ⑨

10 Hotel Copenhagen

Just minutes away from the city centre by Metro, this hotel offers rooms sleeping up to four with shared bathrooms. There are also some rooms with en-suite facilities. Free Internet is available in the reception and breakfast can be ordered when you book for a small additional charge. ◈ *Map E6 • Egilsgade 33, Islands Brygge • 32 96 27 27 • www.hotelcopenhagen. dk* • ⑨

Left **Dansk Bed & Breakfast** Right **Adina Apartment Hotel**

⟨10⟩ Other Accommodation

1 Danhostel Copen-hagen Amager
Four kilometres from the city centre (20 mins by bus), this hostel offers rooms with 2–5 beds, a kitchen, laundry services, Internet access, a TV room, lockers and a children's playground. It is very close to Fields shopping centre. A YHA membership card is required. ◈ *Vejlands Allé 200, Sundbyvester • 32 52 29 08 • Open 2 Jan–15 Dec; check-in: 1–5pm • Dis access • www.danhostel copenhagen.dk • ⊛*

2 Danhostel Copen-hagen Downtown
Located right in the heart of the city, this hostel promises a vibrant and artistic international atmosphere. It has a café, lounge and restaurant. In addition to the dorm and four-bedded rooms, there are rooms for two to three people with en-suite facilities. A YHA membership card is required, which can be bought when checking in. ◈ *Map J5 • Vandkunsten 5 • 70 23 21 10 • www.copenhagen downtown.com • ⊛*

3 STAY Apartment Hotel
A stunning-looking building renovated by the designers of Hay House *(see p68)*, STAY offers serviced apartments with superb waterfront views. The building also houses an Italian restaurant, organic supermarket and gourmet bakery. Vesterbro is a few minutes' walk away. ◈ *Map D6 • Islands Brygge 79A • 72 44 44 34 • www.staycopenhagen.dk • ⊛⊛⊛⊛*

4 YMCA Interpoint
Open only for a short time in the summer, this small hostel (36 beds) is very popular. It is set inside an old house and has a large living room with a piano. The rooms, though small, offer a good garden view and free Internet access. ◈ *Map C5 • Valdemarsgade 15, Vesterbro • 33 31 15 74 • Open Jul–mid-Aug • www. ymca-interpoint.dk • ⊛*

5 City Camp
Centrally located and close to the harbour, this is a good option if you want to park your camper van or caravan while in the city. To make reservations via e-mail *(see below)*, provide your licence plate number and your arrival and departure dates. ◈ *Fisketorvet / Vasbygade, Vesterbro • 21 42 53 84 • Open 1 Jun–1 Sep • Reservations@citycamp.dk • www.citycamp.dk • ⊛*

6 Bellahøj Camping
If you wish to pitch a tent, this is the nearest campsite to town. It is in a residential area, 4.5 km (2½ miles) from the city centre on the 2A bus or a short bike ride. It provides all the basic amenities that are required while camping. ◈ *Hvidkildevej 66 • 38 10 11 50 • Open 1 Jun–31 Aug • www.bellahoj-camping. dk • ⊛*

7 Adina Apartment Hotel
Slightly away from the city centre, this apart-ment hotel offers great facilities, including a gym, baby-sitting services, an indoor heated pool, flat screen TVs and CD players. ◈ *Amerika Plads 7 • 39 69 10 00 • www.adina. eu • ⊛⊛⊛*

8 Apartment in Copenhagen
Agency specializing in short- and long-term lets in smart, furnished apartments at attractive city locations, for couples and for families. ◈ *Map E4 • Hindegade 6 • 77 34 56 45 • www.apartmentin copenhagen.com • ⊛⊛*

9 Dansk Bed & Breakfast
This B&B agency offers good quality private accommodation in central locations. ◈ *Map G4 • Sankt Peders Stræde 41 • 39 61 04 05 • www.bbdk. dk • ⊛*

10 The Hospitality Club
Stay for free and meet a global network of hosts, travellers and locals who aim to increase intercultural understanding. ◈ *www. hospitalityclub.org*

Price Categories

For a standard, double room per night (with breakfast if included), taxes and extra charges.

⑳	up to 700 Dkr
⑳⑳	700–1,000
⑳⑳⑳	1,000–1,200
⑳⑳⑳⑳	1,200–1,600
⑳⑳⑳⑳⑳	over 1,600 Dkr

Left **Admiral** Centre **Scandic Copenhagen**

⑩ Rooms with a View

1 Radisson Blu Royal Hotel

This famous Radisson hotel, designed by Arne Jacobsen in the 1950s, is packed with five-star comforts. The rooms afford great views over the city. On the 20th floor, the well-known Alberto K restaurant serves a fusion of Nordic and Italian cuisine (see p67). ✎ Map G5 • ⑳⑳⑳⑳⑳

2 Copenhagen Island

This state-of-the-art hotel is on an island in the middle of Copenhagen harbour. Architect Kim Utzon's extraordinary building places a great emphasis on the play of glass and light. The rooms offer scenic views of the Sound. It also has its own fitness centre. ✎ Map J6 • Kalvebod Brygge 53 • 33 38 96 00 • www.copen hagenisland.com • ⑳⑳⑳

3 Copenhagen Strand

This three-star hotel is housed in a 1869 harbour-front warehouse, tucked away on a pretty, quiet street opposite the Christianshavns canal. The decor is rustic and the view is wonderful. ✎ Map L4 • Havnegade 37 • 33 48 99 00 • www.copenhagen strand.com • ⑳⑳⑳

4 Admiral

Originally an 18th-century granary, the rooms in this splendid four-star hotel overlook the Sound and offer a stunning view of the Opera House (see p91). Two cannons guard the entrance and the foyer displays some beautiful models of ships. The rooms are very comfort-able and the restaurant, Salt, is excellent. ✎ Map L3 • Toldbodgade 24–8 • 33 74 14 14 • www. admiralhotel.dk • ⑳⑳⑳⑳

5 Hotel CPHLIVING

The world's first floating hotel is located in a boat on the harbour. There are just 12 rooms, all with small balconies and Wi-Fi. A sun deck with deck chairs is available for guests. This is a non-smoking hotel. ✎ Map J6 • Langebrogade 1C • 61 60 85 46 • www. cphliving.com • ⑳⑳⑳

6 Scandic Copenhagen

Standing tall near the Tycho Brahe Planetarium (see p84), it offers magnificent panoramic views over Copenhagen's rooftops. Try out their fabulous breakfasts. For the best rates, check the "Early" and "Flex" deals. ✎ Map C5 • Vester Søgade 6 • 33 14 35 35 • www. scandic-hotels.com/ copenhagen • ⑳⑳⑳⑳

7 Danhostel Copenhagen City

This modern five-star Danhostel is one of the biggest in the city. It is located close to Tivoli and Rådhuspladsen and offers great views over the city's attractions. ✎ Map C5 • H C Andersens Blvd 50 • 33 11 85 85 • Dis access • www.danhostel. dk/copenhagencity • ⑳

8 Skovshoved Hotel

Away from the bustle of central Copenhagen, this elegant seaside hotel is over 350 years old. Tastefully decorated in a Scandinavian style, it is surrounded by fisher-men's houses and offers beautiful views. The restaurant is mentioned in the Michelin Guide. ✎ Map B2 • Strandvejen 267, Charlottenlund • 39 64 00 28 • www.skovshoved hotel.dk • ⑳⑳⑳⑳

9 Skodsborg Kurhotel and Spa

Formerly a summer palace, this century-old health resort is a beautiful place to stay. Overlooking the sea, it is the perfect destination for health and fitness fanatics, offering a range of therapies and fitness programmes. ✎ Skods-borg Strandvej 139, Skods-borg • 45 58 58 00 • www. skodsborg.dk • ⑳⑳⑳⑳

10 Dragør Badehotel

This three-star harbour hotel in the fishing village of Dragør is a popular destination with tourists and boasts rooms with gorgeous views of the sea and the countryside. ✎ Drogdensvej 43, Dragør • 32 53 05 00 • www. badehotellet.dk • ⑳⑳

General Index

Page numbers in **bold** type refer to main entries.

1105 (bar) 70

A

A Closer Grand Canyon (Hockney) 101
A Pair 68
Absalon, Bishop 17, 28, 32, 33, 58, 97
accommodation *see* hotels
Adina Apartment Hotel 116
Admiral 117
admission prices 107
air travel 106
Akimbo 69
Akvarium, Tivoli 11
Albers, Josef 101
Alberto K 67
Alexander III, Tsar 21
Alexander Nevsky Kirke 21, 78
Algade 100
Amager Strandpark 45
Amagertorv 64
Amaliehaven 21, 78
Amalienborg 7, **20–21**, 58, 76, 77
Amigo Bar 54
Ancher, Anna 35
Ancher, Michael 35
Andersen, Hans Christian 15, 18, 19, 38–9, 45, 85
statue 37, 66
Wonderful World of H C Andersen Museum 56, 66
Anthon, G D 89
AOC 48
Apartment in Copenhagen 116
apartments 116
Arken Museum for Moderne Kunst 98
Artemis (Hammershøi) 23
art galleries *see* museums and galleries
artists 35
Assistens Kirkegård 39, 45, 75
Astronomical Clock 63
Atlas Bar 67
ATMs 109
Aurum 92
Avenue Hotel 113

Axel Hotel Guldsmeden 114
Axeltorv 102

B

Baan Suan 80
Babette Guldsmeden 113
Bacon, Francis 97
Bakkehusmuseet 38, 84–5
Bakken Fun Fair 99
Baldaccini, César 101
Baltic Sail 102
Bang & Olufsen 47
Bankeråt 67
banking 109
Bar Rouge 70
bars 43, 50–51, 67, 71, 87, 93
Bastionen + Løven 50, 93
Battles of Copenhagen 33
beaches 45
bed and breakfast 116
beer 53, 84, 85
Bellahøj Camping 116
Bellahøj Svømmestadion 45
Bellevue 45
Bering, Vitus Jonasson 33
Beyond Copenhagen **96–103**
dining 103
Helsingør 102
Louisiana Museum 97, 99, 101
Roskilde 100
bicycles 44, 106
Birger Christensen 68
Bissen, Vilhelm 15, 25
Bit Antik 92
Black Diamond 8, 37
Blixen, Karen 18, 39, 98
Bluetooth, Harald 32, 33, 59
Bodega 81
Bodum 47
Bohr, Niels 33, 45
Bopa 79
Børsen 36, 91
Botanisk Have 75, 77
Bournonville, August 39, 45
Boys' Guard, Tivoli 11
Brahe, Tycho 33
Bredgade 47
Bronze Age artifacts 26
Bror 67
budget travel 111, 115

C

Cab Inn City 115
Cab Inn Express 115
Cab Inn Metro 115
Cab Inn Scandinavia 115
Café Bang & Jensen 85, 87
Café Bomhuset 103
Café Intime 54
Café Jorden Rundt 103
Café Lindevang 87
Café Oscar 79
Café Pavillonen 81
Café Petersborg 71
Cafe Retro 50–51
Café Wilder 91, 93
cafés 43, 50–51, 67, 71, 79, 87, 93, 103
camping 116
canals 9
Canal Tours 44
car hire 106
Caritas Springvandet 37, 66
Carlsberg Brewery 37, 84
Carlton Hotel Guldsmeden 114
Caroline Amelie, Queen 15
Carstensen, Georg 13
castles and palaces
Amalienborg 7, **20–21**, 58, 76, 77
Charlottenborg Slot 19
Christian VII's Palace 20
Christian VIII's Palace 20
Christian IX's Palace 21
Christiansborg Slot 28, 36, 57, 65
Fredensborg Slot 58–9
Frederik VIII's Palace 20
Frederiksberg Slot 84
Frederiksborg Slot 36, 59, 98–9
Kastellet 78
Kronborg Slot 59, 99, 102
Marienlyst Slot 102
Rosenborg Slot 6, **14–15**, 36, 58, 76, 77
Roskilde Palace 100
Trekroner 9
Centralhjørnet 54
Charlie's Bar 71
Charlie Scott's 43
Charlottenborg Slot 19
Charlottenlund Beach 45
Charlottenlund Slotshave 99
children 56–7, 107

Christ as the Suffering Redeemer (Mantegna) 22
Christensen, Helena 39
Christian I 17
Christian II 32, 88
Christian III 32
Christian IV 14–15, 16, 17, 29, 33, 36, 37, 58, 59, 88, 98
Christian IV (hotel) 113
Christian V 15, 18, 37, 59
Christian VI 15, 28, 29
Christian VII 20
Christian VIII 13, 20, 58
Christian IX 21, 58
Christiania 89, 91
Christiania Shop 92
Christians Kirke 40, 89, 91
Christiansborg Slot 28, 36, 58, 65
Christiansborg Slotskirke 29, 41
Christianshavn and Holmen 9, 90, **88–93**
    dining 93
    shopping 92
Christine McKinney Møller Foundation 21
Christmas 11
churches 40–41
    Alexander Nevsky Kirke 21, 78
    Christians Kirke 40, 89, 91
    Christiansborg Slotskirke 29, 41
    Grundtvigs Kirke 41
    Helligåndskirken 16, 17, 40
    Holmens Kirke 37, 41
    Karmeliterklosteret 102
    Kastelskirken 78
    Marmorkirken 21, 41, 76–7
    Roskilde Domkirke 41, 59, 100
    St Albans Kirke 78
    Sankt Olai Kirke 99, 102
    Sankt Petri Kirke 17, 41
    Trinitatis Kirke 17, 40
    Vor Frelsers Kirke 40, 89, 91
    Vor Frue Kirke 17, 39, 40
Cibi e Vini 92
cinemas 111
Cisternerne – Museet for Moderne Glaskunst 85
City Camp 116

climate 107
Club Christopher 54–5
Club Mambo 53, 70
Cnut, King 33
Cofoco 87
Comfort Hotel Vesterbro 114
communications 109
Copencabana Havnebadet ved Fisketorvet 45
Copenhagen Beer Festival 53
Copenhagen Island 117
Copenhagen Jazz Festival 43
Copenhagen Plaza 112
Copenhagen Pride Festival 55
Copenhagen Strand 117
credit cards 109
Crown Jewels 14, 58, 59
cultural figures 39
Culture Box 53
currency 109
customs regulations 107
cycling 44, 106, 110
Cylinda-Line 47

D
Danefae 86
Danhostel Copenhagen Amager 116
Danhostel Copenhagen City 117
Danhostel Copenhagen Downtown 116
Danmarks Teknisk Museum 99, 102
Dansk Bed & Breakfast 116
Dansk Jødisk Museum 29, 34
Davids Samling 34, 76, 77
Degas, Edgar 25
Den Blå Planet 57, 99
dental treatment 108
design companies 47
Designer Zoo 86
Designmuseum Danmark 35, 77
DGI-Byen 45
disabled access 108
discount smartcards 106, 111
Divaen og Krudtuglen 80
doctors 108
Domhus 66
Donaldson, Mary 20
Donn Ya Doll 86
Dragør Badehotel 117

drinking etiquette 110
driving 106, 110
drugs 110
duty free goods 107
Dyrehaven 45

E
Eckersberg, Christoffer 25, 35
Eco Ego 80
Egyptian art 25
Eigtved, Nicolas 20, 40, 41, 89
Elephant Gate, The 37, 84
Eliasson, Olafur 35, 52
Elmgreen & Dragset 23
Emmerys Bakery 50
Empire Bio Cinema 81
English language 110
Era Ora 48, 93
Eric of Pomerania 29
Erik VII 32
etiquette 110
Etruscan art 24
Ewald, Johannes 85
exchange services 109
Experimentarium 57

F
Fælledparken 78
Fælledparkens Soppesø 45
Færgekroen Bryghus 12
Famo 87
Far Eastern artifacts 27
ferries 106
festivals 43, 53, 55, 102
fire (1728) 33
First Hotel Kong Frederik 113
First Hotel Mayfair 114
Fischer 79
Fiskerkrone 37, 65
Fisketorv Shopping Centre 47
flea markets 44
Flora Danica Porcelain 47
La Fontaine 43
food 49
    cheap eats 111
Formel B 49, 87
Fredensborg Slot 58–9
Frederik III 15, 18, 27, 32
Frederik IV 15, 84
Frederik V 15, 21, 37
Frederik VII 32
Frederik VIII 20, 58
Frederik, Crown Prince 20, 58

Frederiks Have 87
Frederiksberg see Vesterbro and Frederiksberg
Frederiksberg Have 83
Frederiksberg Slot 84
Frederiksborg Slot 36, 59, 98–9
Frederiksdal Friluftsbad 45
Frederiksstaden **20–21**
free events 111
Frihedsmuseet 35, 77
Frilandsmuseet 97, 99

G
Gammel Dock 91
Gammel Strand 66
gardens see parks and gardens
Gauguin, Paul 25
gays and lesbians 54–5
Gefährlich 52, 81
Gefionspringvandet 37, 77, 78
Geist 67
Generator Hostel Copenhagen 115
Georg Jensen 68
Georg Jensen Museum 66
Giacometti, Alberto 97, 101
Girlie Hurly 86
La Glace 51
Godt 48
Golden Age 25, 38, 83, 84
Golden Axis 21
Gråbøl, Sofie 39
Gråbrødretorv 17
Grand Hotel 113
Grand Teatret 70
Great Plague 33
Greek art 24
Grill Royal 51
Grønbech & Churchill 48, 79
Grønlykke 69
Grundtvigs Kirke 41
Guggenheim, Harry 101
Guinness World Records Museum 56, 66
Den Gule Cottage 103
Gundestrup Cauldron 26

H
Hadid, Zaha 98
Haile Selassie, Emperor 19
Hallager, Thora 39
Halmtorvet 85
Halvandet 90
Hamlet Festival 102
Hammershøi, Vilhelm 23, 35

Hanseatic League 28, 32
harbour buses 8, 106
Harbour Sights 6, **8–9**
Harsdorff, Caspar Frederik 21
Hatton, Denys Finch 98
Haven, Lambert van 89
Havnebadet 9, 45
Hay House 68
health 108
Helligåndskirken 16, 17, 40
Helsingør 97, 99, 102
Helsingør Bymuseum 99, 102
Henningsen, Poul 39, 47
Henrik, Prince Consort 21
Henrik Vibskov 69
Hereford Beefstouw 13
Hestetorvet 100
Hilbert København 92
Hilton Copenhagen Airport 112
Den Hirschsprungske Samling 35, 75, 77
historic buildings 36–7
history 32
Hive 52
Hockney, David 101
Højbro Plads 17
Holberg, Ludvig 17
Holmen see Christianshavn and Holmen
Holmens Kirke 37, 41
Hospitality Club, The 116
hospitals 108
hostels 116
Hotel Alexandra 112
Hotel Copenhagen 115
Hotel CPHLIVING 117
Hotel d'Angleterre 18, 19, 39, 112
Hotel Front 112
Hotel Sct. Thomas 115
Hotel SP34 113
Hotel Twentyseven 113
hotels 112–17
  budget 115
  expensive 113
  luxury 112
  mid-range 114
  rooms with a view 117
houseboats 9
Humlebæk 99
Huset-KBH 43
Husmanns Vinstue 67, 71
Hviids Vinstue 71

I
Ibsens Hotel 114
Ida Davidsen 79
Ideal Bar 53
Illum Department Store 68
Illums Bolighus 68
Imperial Hotel 113
Impressionists 25, 98
Inblik 92
Inderhavnen 8, 89
Ingrid, Queen Dowager 20
insurance 108
Internet access 109
Inuit culture 27
Italia-La Vecchia Signora 13

J
Jacobsen, Arne 39, 47, 83, 103
Jacobsen, Jacob 59, 84, 85, 98
Jacobsen, Robert 85
Jailhouse 54
Det Japanske Tårn 12
jaywalking 110
jazz venues and events 42, 43, 102
Jazzcup 43
Jazzhouse 42, 70
Jazzhus Montmartre 43, 70
Jensen, Georg 47, 66, 68
Jews 29, 33, 34
Jorn, Asger 23, 35, 97, 101
Juice 80

K
Kaare Klint Furniture 47
Karen Blixen Museum 98, 99
Karmeliterklosteret 102
Karriere Bar 52
Kastellet 78
Kastelskirken 78
Kate's Joint 79
Kierkegaard, Søren 29, 32, 33
Kirkeby, Per 23, 85, 97
Kirkegård 100
Kjærholm furniture 47
Klædebo 80
Klampenborg 99
Klaus Samsøe 86
Klint, Kaare 47
Klint, PV Jensen 41
Københavns Museum 83, 85
Køge Bugt 98

Køge Bugt Strandpark 45
Koncerthuset 43
Kong Arthur 113
Kong Hans Kælder 48
Kongelige
    Afstøbningssamling 78
Det Kongelige Teater 19,
    38, 42
Kongens Have 6, **14–15**,
    45, 76
Kongens Nytorv 7, **18–19**,
    64–5
Krogs Fiskerestaurant 67
Kronborg Slot 59, 99, 102
Kronprinsensgade 46
Krøyer, Peder Severin 35
Kunstforeningen Gammel
    Strand 64

L
Lagkagehuset 92
L'Alsace 67
L'Altro 93
Langelinie 8
Larsen, Henning 64, 91
Latin Quarter 6, **16–17**, 64
Laundromat Café 50
Lego 47
Libeskind, Daniel 29
Lichtenstein, Roy 101
Liebe 69
Lille Kongensgade 1 39
Lille Strandstræde 19
Lippi, Filippino 23
Little Mermaid, The 9, 37,
    77, 78
lost property 108
Lot, The 70
Louisiana Museum 97, 99,
    101
Lukow-Nielsen, Henry 37
Luna's Diner 93
Lund, Søren 98
Lurblæserne 37

M
Mads Nørgaard 68
Magasin du Nord 19, 38, 69
magazines 107, 109
Manet, Edouard 25, 101
Mantegna, Andrea 22
Marc by Marc Jacobs 69
Le Marché Deli Takeaway
    86
Margrethe, Queen 21, 58
Margrethe I, Queen 58, 59
Marie Dagmar, Tsarina 21
Marienlyst Slot 102
Maritime Festival 102

Marmorkirken 21, 41, 76–7
Mary, Crown Princess 20
Masken Bar & Café 55
Matisse, Henri 23, 25
Mazzoli's Caffe & Trattoria 12
medical treatment 108
Medicinsk Museion 78
The Meeting of Joachim
    and Anne (Lippi) 23
Meet the Danes 49
Meet Gay Copenhagen 55
Meldahl, Ferdinand 41
Mens Bar 55
Mexibar 81
Meyers Deli 86
microbreweries 53
Mikkelsen, Mads 39
Mix Copenhagen Film
    Festival 55
Mo Christianshavn 92
mobile phones 109
Modigliani, Amedeo 23
Mojo Bluesbar 42
Møller, AP 21
Møller, Mærsk McKinney
    91
Moltke, Adam Gottlob 20
Monday closing 110
Mondo Kaos 80
Moore, Henry 101
Mortensen, Richard 35
Mortensen, Viggo 39
Mother 87
movies 111
Mumm 103
Munk, Kirsten 15
Munthe 69
museums and galleries
    34–5
    Amber Museum 19
    Arken Museum for
        Moderne Kunst 98
    Bakkehusmuseet 38,
        84–5
    Carlsberg Brewery 84
    Cisternerne – Museet for
        Moderne Glaskunst 85
    Danmarks Teknisk
        Museum 99, 102
    Dansk Jødisk Museum
        29, 34
    Davids Samling 34, 76, 77
    Designmuseum
        Danmark 35, 77
    Frihedsmuseet 35, 77
    Frilandsmuseet 97
    Georg Jensen Museum
        66

museums and galleries
    (cont.)
    Guinness World Records
        Museum 56, 66
    Helsingør Bymuseum
        99, 102
    Den Hirschsprungske
        Samling 35, 75, 77
    Karen Blixen Museet 98,
        99
    Københavns Museum
        83, 85
    Kongelige
        Afstøbningssamling 78
    Louisiana Museum 97,
        99, 101
    Maritime Museum of
        Denmark 102
    Medicinsk Museion 78
    Nationalmuseet 7, **26–7**,
        34, 56, 64, 65
    Ny Carlsberg Glyptotek
        7, **24–5**, 34, 63, 65
    Odrupgaard 98, 99
    Orlogsmuseet 90, 91
    Post & Telemuseet 66
    Ripley's Believe It or
        Not! 57
    Roskilde Museum 100
    Roskilde Palace 100
    Statens Museum for
        Kunst 7, **22–3**, 34, 56,
        75, 77
    Storm P Museet 84
    Teatermuseet 28, 35, 65
    Thorvaldsens Museum
        29, 35
    Tøjhusmuseet 29, 56
    Vikingeskibsmuseet 100
    Wonderful World of H C
        Andersen 56, 66
music
    free events 111
    venues 42–3
Musicon 100

N
Nansensgade 46
Nationalmuseet 7, **26–7**,
    34, 56, 64, 65
newspapers 109
Nielsen, Carl 39
Nielsen, Kai 25
nightlife 52–3, 70, 81
Nimb Brasserie 12
Nimb Hotel 11, 112
Nimb Terrasse 12
Noa Noa 68

Noma 49, 93
Nord Natklub 53
Nørgaard, Bjørn 9, 35, 64
Normann Copenhagen 80
Nørrebro, Østerbro & North
  of Gothersgade **74–81**
  dining 79
  nightlife 81
  shopping 80
North Atlantic House 90
Ny Carlsberg Glyptotek 7,
  24–5, 34, 63, 65
Det Ny Teater 43
Nyhavn 7, 8, **18–19**, 64–5
Nyhavn 71 (hotel) 112
Nyhavn Nos 20, 67 and 18
  18, 38
Nyhavns Glaspusteri 80
Nyrop, Martin 63

O
Oak Room, The 81
Odrupgaard 98, 99
Oehlenschläger, Adam 85
Øksnehallen 90
Oldenburg Horn 59
Olsen, Jens 63
Open-Air Stage (Tivoli) 11
opening hours 107
Opera (hotel) 114
Operaen (Opera House)
  8, 37, 42, 77, 90–91
Orangeriet Kongens Have 79
Order of the Danneborg 59
Order of the Elephant 59
Øresund 8, 89
Øresundsakvariet 102
Orlogsmuseet 90, 91
Ørsted, Hans Christian 33
Oscar Bar and Café 54
outdoor activities 44–5
outdoor dining 44
Oven Vande Café 93
Overgaden Neden Vandet 90
Overgaden Oven Vandet
  90, 91

P
Palace Guards 21
Palace Hotel 112
palaces see castles and
  palaces
Pang Christianshavn 92
Pan Idraet 55
Pantomime Theatre 11
Paradise Genetically
  Altered 9
Park Diskotek 52, 81

Parken 43
parking 106
parks and gardens
  Amaliehaven 21
  Botanisk Have 75, 77
  Charlottenlund Slotshave
    99
  Dyrehaven 45
  Fælledparken 78
  Frederiksberg Have 83
  Kirkegård 100
  Kongens Have 6, **14–15**,
    45, 76
  Louisiana Museum 97,
    99, 101
  Royal Library Gardens 29
  Tivoli 6, **10–13**, 57
  Winter Garden 24, 25, 65
  Zoologisk Have 45, 57, 83
Peblinge Sø 45
Pedersen, Carl-Henning 35
Penthouse 70
Perch's Tea Room 71
performing arts venues
  42–3
personal safety 108
Peter the Great 16
pharmacies 108
Phoenix 113
Picasso, Pablo 97, 101
Please, Keep Quiet!
  (Elmgreen & Dragset) 23
police 108
porcelain 47, 58
Porte à Gauche 92
Post & Telemuseet 66
Post-Impressionists 25
postal services 109
prehistoric artifacts 27
prices 107, 111
Props Coffee Shop 81
public holidays 107
public transport 106, 110
Pussy Galore's Flying
  Circus 50, 79, 81

R
Rabes Have 50, 93
Rådhuset 63
Rådhuspladsen 66
radio 109
Radisson Blu Falconer 114
Radisson Blu Royal Hotel
  83, 117
Radisson Blu Scandinavia
  112
Rahbek, Kamma Lyhne 38,
  84

Rahbek, Knud 38, 84
rail travel 106
Rainbow Festival 55
Rasmussen, Knud 33
Reformation 32
Refshaleøen 90
Regensen 17, 36
reservations 111
Restaurant Gilleleje Havn
  103
Restaurant Klubben 87
Restaurant Peder Oxe 67
Restaurant Sletten 103
Restaurant Zeleste 79
restaurants 48–9
  Beyond Copenhagen 103
  cheap eats 111
  Christianshavn and
    Holmen 93
  Nørrebro, Østerbro &
    North of Gothersgade 79
  Tivoli 12–13
  Tivoli North to
    Gothersgade 67, 71
  Vesterbro and
    Frederiksberg 87
rickshaws 106
Ripley's Believe It or Not!
  57
RizRaz Sticks 'n' Veggies
  67
road travel 106
Rockahula 86
Den Røde Cottage 103
Roman art 24
Romantic Paintings
  (Kirkeby) 23
Rosenborg Slot 6, **14–15**,
  36, 58, 76, 77
Roskilde 97, 100
Roskilde Domkirke 41, 59,
  100
Roskilde Kloster 100
Roskilde Museum 100
Roskilde Palace 100
Roskilde, Treaty of 32
Royal Copenhagen
  Porcelain 58, 68
royal family 110
  see also kings and
    queens by name
royal sights 58–9
Royal Smushi Café 71
Royal Stables 28
royal yacht 9
Ruby 70
Rundetårn 16, 36, 38–9, 65
Rust 52, 81

S

sailing 45
St Albans Church 78
Salonen 51
Salt Bar and Restaurant 79
Saly, Jacques 21, 37
Sand 68
Sankt Jørgens Sø 44–5
Sankt Olai Kirke (Helsingør Domkirke) 99, 102
Sankt Petri (hotel) 112
Sankt Petri Kirke 17, 41
SAS Radisson Royal Hotel 36
Savoy 114
Scandic Copenhagen 117
seasons 107
security 108
self-catering 116
shopping 46–7
  Christianshavn and Holmen 92
  Nørrebro, Østerbro & North of Gothersgade 80
  Strøget 68
  Vesterbro and Frederiksberg 86
Skindbuksen 71
Skodsborg Kurhotel and Spa 117
Skomagergade 100
Skovshoved Hotel 117
Sleep In Green 116
Slotsholmen 7, 28–9, 65
Slotskælderen hos Gitte Kik 71
Sneaky Fox 69
Snekken 103
Sofiekælderen 93
Søllerod Kro 103
Le Sommelier 49
son-et-lumière (Tivoli) 11
Søpavillonen 52
Sophie Amalie, Queen 27
Sophie Magdalene, Queen 59
Den Sorte Diamant 8, 37
Sortedam Sø 45
Søstrene Olsen 103
Spiseloppen 93
Square, The 114
Stændertorvet 100
Standard, The 43
Statens Museum for Kunst 7, 22–3, 34, 56, 75, 77
statues 37
STAY Apartment Hotel 116
Stengade 99, 102

Sticks 'n' Sushi 87
Stilleben 69
Store Strandstræde 19
Storm P Museet 84
Strandgade 99, 102
Strøget 46, 66
Studenterhuset 70
Sunset Jazz Festival 102
Susanne Juul 80
Sweden
  rudeness about 110
  wars with 32
Sweyn I Forkbeard 32
swimming pools 45
Synagogen 16

T

Tage Andersen Boutique & Museum 80
Tango y Vinos 43
taxis 106
Teatermuseet 28, 35
telephone services 109
television 109
Thé à la Menthe 51
theft 108
Thorvaldsen, Bertel 29, 35
Thorvaldsens Museum 29, 35
Tietgen, Carl Frederik 41
Tiger Lily 86
tipping 111
Tivoli 6, 10–13, 44, 57, 63, 65
Tivoli Concert Hall 11, 42
Tivoli Hotel 114
Tivoli North to Gothersgade 62–71
  dining 67, 71
  nightlife 70
  shopping 68–9
Tøjhusmuseet 29, 56
Torvegade 91
Torvehallerne Kbh 47
tourist information 107
transport 106
Trekroner 9
Trier, Lars von 39
Trinitatis Kirke 17, 40
Les Trois Cochons 85, 87
Dan Turéll 71
Tycho Brahe Planetarium 84

U

Umami 48
Universitetet (University of Copenhagen) 17, 32, 64

V

Værnedamsvej 86
Valdemar I 32
Van Gogh, Vincent 25
Vandkunsten Sandwich Bar 71
VEGA 43, 53
Vela 54
Vesterbro and Frederiksberg 82–7
  dining 87
  shopping 86
Vikingeskibsmuseet 100
Vikings 27, 100
Vingårdsstræde 6 19, 38
Vipp 47
visas 107
Vor Frelsers Kirke 40, 89, 91
Vor Frue Kirke 17, 39, 40, 58

W

Wagamama 12
WakeUp Copenhagen Borgergade 115
WakeUp Copenhagen Carsten Niebuhrs 115
walking 106
walking tours
  Christianshavn and Holmen 91
  Nørrebro, Østerbro & North of Gothersgade 77
  Tivoli North to Gothersgade 65
  Vesterbro and Frederiksberg 85
Wallmans Cirkusbygningen 42
Warhol, Andy 101
Wettergren & Wettergren 69
Winter Garden 24, 25, 65
Winter Jazz 43
Wonderful World of HC Andersen Museum 56, 66
Woodhouse 12
World War II 33

Y

YMCA Interpoint 116
youth hostels 116

Z

Zleephotel Hotel Copenhagen City 115
Zoologisk Have 45, 57, 83

Acknowledgments

The Author
Antonia Cunningham would like to thank the following for their help and support while researching and writing this book:
Henrik Thierlein at Wonderful Copenhagen, Annette Wæber of Meet the Danes and Bodil and Troels Joergensen and their family for their kind hospitality; Hotel Square, No 71, Admiral Hotel, Bertrams Hotel Guldmedsen; Annette Larsen, Caroline Disum and Louise Albeck at Café Rabes Have; Mads Grimstad and Nina Wengel at the Opera House and Brian at Barcelona for their helpful advice; Nicolaj Steen Møller for his comments and advice; and all the staff who kindly showed me around hotels and restaurants and provided information. I would also especially like to thank Nick Simpson, Susan Hazledine, my sister Francesca Mitchell and my editor Fay Franklin, who was very understanding of my pregnant state and the odd delay that went with it.

Photographer Jon Spaull

Fact checking and additional text
Jane Graham, Nikolaj Steen Møller, Laura Pilgaard Rasmussen

AT DORLING KINDERSLEY

Publisher Douglas Amrine

Publishing Manager
Scarlett O'Hara

Design Manager Karen Constanti

Senior Cartographic Designer
Casper Morris

Senior Editor Fay Franklin

Project Editor Alastair Laing

DTP Designer Natasha Lu

DK Picture Library Romaine Werblow, Rose Horridge

Senior Picture Researchers
Taiyaba Khatoon, Ellen Root

Picture Researchers Marta Bescos, Sumita Khatwan, Rhiannon Furbear

Production Linda Dare

AT CREATIVE QUOTIENT
(A Repro Enterprise)

Art Director Asha Madhavan

Editors Shantala Bellare, Gauri Kelkar

Designer Dinesh Kashyap

Project Managers Deepali Salvi, Jatin Mehta

Additional Editorial and Design
Louise Abbott, Emma Anacootee, Tessa Bindloss, Imogen Corke, Simon Davis, Jane Graham, Lydia Halliday, Integrated Publishing Solutions, Lisa Jacobs, Bharti Karakoti, Sumita Khatwani, Priya Kukadia, Hayley Maher, Marianne Petrou, Alison McGill, Helen Peters, Christine Stroyan, Sylvia Tombesi-Walton, Catherine Waring, Sophie Wright, Conrad van Dyk

Additional Photography Demetrio Carrasco, Dorota and Mariusz Jarymowiczowie, Rough Guides/Roger Norum

Picture Credits
Key: a-above; b-below/bottom; c-centre; f-far; l-left; r-right; t-top.

The Publisher would like to thank the following for their kind assistance and permission to photograph their establishments:

2nd Birkegade, Amalienborg Slot, Birger Christensen, Café Ketchup, Café Ultimo, Centralhjørnet, Christiansborg Slot, Christians Kirke, Club Mambo, Copenhagen Admiral Hotel, Copenhagen Jazz House, Copenhagen Zoo, Culture Box, Danmarks Akvarium, Dansk Jødisk Museum, Designer Zoo, Det Nationalhistoriske Museum på Frederiksborg Slot, Hillerød, Emmerys, Experimentarium, Formel B, Frederiks Kirke (Marmorkirken), Gefährlich, La Glace, Guinness World Records Museum, Hotel Fox, Illums Bolighus, Jailhouse Event Bar/Restaurant, Kunstindustrimuseet, The Laundromat Café, Louisiana Museum, Magasin du Nord, Masken Bar & Café, Mojo Blues Bar, Museum Erotica, Nationalmuseet, Ny Carlsberg Glyptotek, Operaen, Orlogsmuseet, The Paul, Pussy

Galore's Flying Circus, Rosenborg Slot, Roskilde Museum, Rundetårn, Sneaky Fox, Søpavillonen, Sofiekælderen, Søstrene Olsen, The Square Copenhagen, Tage Anderson, Teatermuseet i Hofteatret, Thé à la Menthe, Tivoli, Vikingeskibsmuseet, Vor Frue Kirke, Zoo Bar.

Works of art have been reproduced with the kind permission of the following copyright holders: Henry Moore, *Two Piece Reclining Figure No. 5, 1963–64* (LH 517) © The Henry Moore Foundation 101tr.

The publisher would like to thank the following individuals, companies and picture libraries for their kind permissions to reproduce their photographs:

4CORNERS IMAGES: SIME / Mezzanotte Susy 94–5.

ALAMY IMAGES: Meritzo 109tl; nagelestock.com 72–3; Realimage 74cl, VIEW Pictures Ltd 99tl; AVENUE HOTEL: 114tr.

CLARION COLLECTION HOTEL MAYFAIR: 114tl; COPENHAGEN JAZZ HOUSE: 70tl; CORBIS: Archivo Iconografico, S.A. 33tl, 33tr.

DANSK DESIGN CENTER: 62cra; DK IMAGES: David Borland 96tr; Rough Guides/Helena Smith 66tl.

ECO EGO: 80tl.

FREDERIKSBORG SLOT: Larsen Lennart 32t; Hans Petersen 32br.

HOTEL COPENHAGEN: 115tl; HVIIDPHOTOGRAPHY: Nimb Terrasse: Anders Hvidd 12tl.

INTOXICA BAR-TIKI BAR & KITCHEN: 70tr

OLDR"ICH KARASEK: 20–21c.

LONELY PLANET IMAGES: Anders Blomqvist 60–61.

MADKLUBBEN TIVOLI: 12tc; THE MARITIME MUSEUM OF DENMARK: Thijs Wolzak 102 tl; MAZZOLI'S CAFFÈ & TRATTORIA: 12tr; MEYERS DELI: 86tr; MO CHRISTIANSHAVN: 92tl; MUSEET SKIBSKLARERERGAARDEN: 102tl.

NATIONALMUSEET: 7clb, 26cr, 26br, 27tl, 27bl, 27cra; NIKOLAJ STEEN MØLLER: 71tl; NY CARLSBERG GLYPTOTEK: 24cb, 25clb.

ORDRUPGAARD: 96tl.

ROSENBORG SLOT: 15ca, 74tl; RUBY COCKTAIL BAR: Mads Jensen 70tr; RUST: 51br, 81tl.

THE SQUARE: 114TR; STATENS MUSEUM FOR KUNST: 22c, 22bc, 23tr, 23c; STRÖMMA DANMARK A/S: 44cla; SUPERSTOCK: Brian Lawrence 4–5.

TIVOLI: 10–11c, 43tl.

VISIT DENMARK: 3bl, 38tc, 10cla; Ireneusz Cyranek 34tr; Danmarks Turistrad 102tl; Bob Krist 34bl; Nicolai Perjesi 34tc; Ukendt 6ca.

WONDERFUL COPENHAGEN: 70tr, 107tr, 116tr, 117c.

All other images © Dorling Kindersley.

For further information see: www.dkimages.com.

Phrase Book

In an Emergency

Help!	**Hjælp!**	yellb!
Stop!	**Stands!**	stanns!
Can you call a doctor?	**Kan du ringe til en læge?**	kann do ringe-til ehn laiyeh?
Can you call an ambulance?	**Kan du ringe til en ambulance?**	kann do ringe-til ehn ahm-boo-lang-seh?
Can you call the police?	**Kan du ringe til politiet?**	kann do ringe-til po-ly-tee'd?
Can you call the fire brigade?	**Kan du ringe til brand-væsenet?**	kann do ringe-til brahn-vaiys-ned?
Is there a telephone here?	**Er der en telefon i nærheden?**	e-ah dah ehn tele-fohn ee neya-hethen?
Where is the nearest hospital?	**Hvor er det nærmeste hospital?**	voa e-ah deh neh-meste hoh-spee-tahl

Useful Phrases

Sorry	**Undskyld**	ons-gull
Goodnight	**Godnat**	goh-nad
Goodbye	**Farvel**	fah-vell
Good evening	**Godaften**	goh-ahf-tehn
Good morning	**Godmorgen**	goh-moh'n
Good morning (after about 9am)	**Goddag**	goh-dah
Yes	**Ja**	yah
No	**Nej**	nye
Please	**Værsgo/ Velbekomme**	vehs-goh/ vell-beh-commeh
Thank you	**Tak**	tahgg
How are you?	**Hvordan har du det?/ Hvordan går det?**	voh-dann hah do deh?/ voh-dan go deh?
Well, thank you	**Godt, tak**	gohd, tahgg
Pleased to have met you	**Det var rart at møde dig**	deh vah rahd add meutheh die
See you!	**Vi ses!**	vee sehs!
I understand	**Jeg forstår**	yay fuh-stoah
I don't understand	**Jeg forstår ikke**	yay fuh-stoah egge
Does anyone speak English?	**Er der nogen, der kan tale engelsk?**	e-ah dah noh-enn dah kann tah-leh eng-ellsgg?
good	**god**	guth
bad	**dårlig**	doh-lee
up	**op**	ohb
down	**ned**	neth
near	**tæt på**	taid poh
far	**langt fra**	lahngd fra
on the left	**til venstre**	till vehn-streh
on the right	**til højre**	till hoy-reh
open	**åben**	oh-ben
closed	**lukket**	luh-geth
warm	**varm**	vahm
cold	**kold**	koll
big	**stor**	stoah
little	**lille**	lee-leh

Making a Telephone Call

Whom am I speaking to?	**Hvem taler jeg med?**	vemm talah yay meth?
I would like to call…	**Jeg vil gerne ringe til…**	yay vill geh-neh ring-eh till…
I will telephone again	**Jeg ringer en gang til**	yay ring-ah ehn gahng till

In a Hotel

Do you have double rooms?	**Findes her dobbelt-værelser?**	feh-ness he-ah dob-belld vah-hel-sah?
With bathroom	**Med bade-værelse**	meth bah-the-vah-hel-sah
With washbasin	**Med hånd-vask**	meth hohn-vasgg
key	**nøgle**	noy-leh
I have a reservation	**Jeg har en reservation**	yay hah ehn res-sah-vah-shohn

Sightseeing

entrance	**indgang**	ehn-gahng
exit	**udgang**	ooth-gahng
exhibition	**udstilling**	ooth-stelling
tourist information	**turisto-plysning**	tooh-reesd-ohb-lehs-ning
town/city hall	**rådhus**	rahd-hus
post office	**posthus**	posd-hus
cathedral	**domkirke**	dom-kia-keh
church	**kirke**	kia-keh
museum	**museum**	muh-seh-uhm
town bus	**bybus**	bih-boos
long-distance bus	**rutebil**	roo-teh-beel
railway station	**banegård**	hah-neh-goh
airport	**lufthavn**	luhft-havn
train	**tog**	toh
ferry terminal	**færgehavn**	fah-veh-havn
bus stop	**busstoppested**	buhs-sdob-beh-steth
long-distance bus station	**rutebilstation**	roo-teh-beel-sta-shion
a public toilet	**et offentligt toilet**	ehd off-end-ligd toa-led

Shopping

I wish to buy…	**Jeg vil gerne købe…**	yay vill geh-neh kyh-beh…
Do you have…?	**Findes der…?**	feh-ness de-ah…?
How much does it cost?	**Hvad koster det?**	vath koh-stah deh
expensive	**dyr**	dyh-ah
cheap	**billig**	billy
size	**størrelse**	stoh-ell-seh
general store	**købmand**	keuhb-mann
greengrocer	**grønthandler**	grund-handla
supermarket	**supermarked**	suh-pah-mah-keth
market	**marked**	mah-keth

Eating Out

Do you have a table for… people?	**Har I et bord til… personer?**	hah ee ed boah till… peh-soh-nah?
I would like to	**Jeg vil gerne**	yay vill geh-neh

sit by the window	**sidde ved vinduet**	saithe veth veen-do-ed
I wish to order...	**Jeg vil gerne bestille...**	yay vill geh-neh beh-stilleh...
I'm a vegetarian	**Jeg er vegetar**	yay eh-ah veh-gehta
children's menu	**børnemenu**	byeh-neh-meh-nye
daily special	**dagens ret**	dayens rad
starter	**forret**	foh-red
main course	**hovedret**	hoh-veth-red
dessert	**dessert**	deh-seh'd
wine list	**vinkort**	veen-cod
sweet	**sødt**	sodt
sour	**surt**	suad
spicy	**stærkt**	stehgd
May I have the bill?	**Må jeg bede om regningen?**	moh yay beh-theh uhm rahy-ning-ehn

Menu Decoder

agurk	**cucumber**	a-guag
ananas	**pineapple**	a-nah-nas
appelsin	**orange**	abbel-seen
blomme	**plum**	blum-ma
brød	**bread**	bruth
champignon	**mushroom**	sham-pee-ong
danskvand	**mineral water**	dansg vann
fersken	**peach**	fes-gehn
fisk	**fish**	fesgg
fløde	**cream**	flu-theh
gulerod	**carrot**	gooleh-roth
grøntsager	**vegetables**	grunn-saha
hummer	**lobster**	humma
is	**ice cream**	ees
kaffe	**coffee**	kah-feh
kartofler	**potatoes**	kah-toff-lah
kød	**meat**	kuth
kylling	**chicken**	killing
kål	**cabbage**	kohl
laks	**salmon**	lahggs
lam	**lamb**	lahm
leverpostej	**liver paté**	leh-vah-poh-stie
løg	**onion**	loy
mælk	**milk**	mailgg
oksekød	**beef**	ogg-seh-kuth
ost	**cheese**	ossd
peber	**pepper**	peh-ba
porre	**leek**	po-a
purløj	**chives**	poo-a-luy
pølse	**sausage**	pill-seh
rejer	**shrimps**	rah-yah
ris	**rice**	rees
rødspætte	**plaice**	roth-speh-da
røget fisk	**smoked fish**	roy-heth fesgg
saftevand	**squash**	sah-fteh-vann
salat	**salad**	sah-lad
salt	**salt**	sald
sild	**herring**	sil
skaldyr	**shellfish**	sgall-dya
skinke	**ham**	sgeng-geh
smør	**butter**	smuah
sodavand	**fizzy drink**	sodah-vann
steg	**steak**	stie
svinekød	**pork**	svee-neh-kuth
syltetøj	**jam**	sill-teh-toi
te	**tea**	teh
tærte	**quiche/pie**	te-ah-teh

torsk	**cod**	tohsgg
vand	**water**	vann
wienerbrød	**Danish pastry**	vee-nah-bryd
æble	**apple**	eh-bleh
æg	**egg**	egg
øl	**beer**	uhl

Time

today	**i dag**	ee-day
tomorrow	**i morgen**	ee-mohn
yesterday	**i går**	ee-goh
before noon	**formiddag**	foh-medday
afternoon	**eftermiddag**	ehftah-medday
evening	**aften**	ahftehn
night	**nat**	nadd
minute	**minut**	meh-nude
hour	**time**	tee-meh
week	**uge**	oo-eh
month	**måned**	moe-neth
year	**år**	oah

Days of the Week

Monday	**mandag**	mann-day
Tuesday	**tirsdag**	teahs-day
Wednesday	**onsdag**	uns-day
Thursday	**torsdag**	toahs-day
Friday	**fredag**	frey-day
Saturday	**lørdag**	lur-day
Sunday	**søndag**	son-day

Months

January	**januar**	ya-nuah
February	**februar**	fib-buah
March	**marts**	mahds
April	**april**	apreal
May	**maj**	mai
June	**juni**	yoo-nee
July	**juli**	yoo-lee
August	**august**	auw-guhsd
September	**september**	sehb-tem-bah
October	**oktober**	ogg-toh-bah
November	**november**	noh-vem-bah
December	**december**	deh-sem-bah

Numbers

0	**nul**	noll
1	**en**	ehn
2	**to**	toh
3	**tre**	tray
4	**fire**	fee-ah
5	**fem**	femm
6	**seks**	seggs
7	**syv**	siu
8	**otte**	oh-deh
9	**ni**	nee
10	**ti**	tee
20	**tyve**	tyh-veh
30	**tredive**	traith-veh
40	**fyrre**	fyr-reh
50	**halvtreds**	hahl-traiths
60	**tres**	traiths
70	**halvfjerds**	hahl-fyads
80	**firs**	fee-ahs
90	**halvfems**	hahl-femms
100	**hundrede**	hoon-dreh-the
200	**tohundrede**	toh-hoon-dreh-the
1,000	**tusind**	tooh-sin-deh
2,000	**totusinde**	toh-tooh-sin-deh

Selected Street Index

Åbnerå	J3	Holmens Kanal	K4	Overgaden Oven Vandet	L5
Åboulevard	C4	Hvitfeldts Stræde	H3	Peder Skrams Gade	L4
Admiralgade	K4	Hyskenstræde	J4	Pile Allé	A5
Ågade	B4	Ingerslevsgade	C6	Pilestræde	J4
Ahlefeldtsgade	H3	Islands Brygge	E6	Platanvej	B5
Allégade	B5	Israels Plads	H3	Polititorvet	H6
Amager Boulevard	E6	Istedgade	C6	Porthusgade	J5
Amagerbrogade	F6	Jagtvej	C2	Prins Jørgens Gård	J5
Amagerfælledvej	F6	Jarmers Plads	G4	Prinsessegade	M5
Amagertorv	J4	Jernbanegade	G5	Pustervig	J3
Amaliegade	L3	Kristen Bernikowsgade	K4	Rådhuspladsen	H5
Applebysplads	K6	Kalkbrænderihavnsgade	F2	Rådhusstræde	J5
Artillerivej	E6	Kalvebod Brygge	J6	Rantzausgade	C4
Asylgade	K4	Kattesundet	H4	Reventlowsgade	G6
Axeltorv	G5	Klareboderne	J4	Rigensgade	K2
Badstuestræde	J4	Klosterstræde	J4	Rolighedsvej	B4
Bånegardsplads	G5	Knabrostræde	J4	Rosenborggade	J3
Bernstorffsgade	G6	Købmagergade	J4	Rosengården	H3
Blegdamsvej	D3	Kompagnistræde	J5	Rosenørns Allé	C4
Bodenhoffs Plads	M5	Kongens Nytorv	K4	Roskildevej	A5
Borgergade	K3	Kristianiagade	E3	Sankt Annæ Gade	L6
Børsgade	K5	Kronprinsengade	J4	Sankt Annæ Plads	L3
Bredgade	L3	Kronprinsessegade	K3	Sankt Peders Stræde	H4
Bremerholm	K4	Krøyers Plads	L5	Silkegade	J4
Brolæggerstræde	J4	Krystalgade	H4	Skindergade	J4
Bryggergade	H5	Kultorvet	J3	Slots Plads	K5
Bülowsvej	B4	Læderstræde	J4	Slotsholmsgade	K5
Christians Brygge	J6	Laksegade	K4	Slutterigade	H5
Christmas Møllers Plads	F6	Landemærket	J3	Smallegade	A4
Dag Hammarskjölds Allé	E3	Langebrogade	K6	Snaregade	J5
Danasvej	C4	Larsens Plads	L3	Sølvgade	J2
Dronningens Tværgade	K3	Larslejsstræde	H4	Sølvtorvet	H2
Dybbølsbro	C6	Lavendelstræde	H5	Sønder Boulevard	C6
Dybbølsgade	C6	Lille Kongensgade	K4	Søndre Fasanvej	A5
Dybensgade	K4	Lille Triangel	E2	Søtorvet	G2
Dyrkøb	H4	Løngangstræde	H5	Store Strandstræde	L4
Enghavevej	B6	Lyngbyvej	D1	Stengade	C3
Esplanaden	L2	Lyrskovgade	B6	Stockholmsgade	J1
Fælledvej	C3	Madvigs Allé	B5	Store Kannikestræde	J4
Falkoner Allé	B4	Magstræde	J5	Store Kirkestræde	K4
Farvergade	H5	Møntergade	J3	Store Kongensgade	K3
Finsensvej	A4	Niels Hemmingsens Gade	J4	Stormgade	J5
Fiolstræde	H3	Nansensgade	G3	Strandboulevarden	E1
Folke Bernadottes Allé	K1	Nicolai Eigtveds Gade	K6	Strandgade	L5
Fortunstræde	K4	Niels Juels Gade	K5	Strøget	J4
Fredensgade	D3	Nikolajgade	K4	Studiestræde	H4
Fredericiagade	L2	Nina Bangs Plads	J3	Tagensvej	C2
Frederiksberg Allé	B5	Njalsgade	E6	Teglgårdsstræde	H4
Frederiksberggade	H5	Nordre Fasanvej	A4	Tietgensgade	G6
Frederiksborggade	G2	Nordre Frihavnsgade/Islands	E2	Tøjhusgade	J5
Frederiksholms Kanal	J5	Nørre Allé	D3	Toldbodgade	L3
Fridtjof Nansens Plads	E2	Nørre Farimagsgade	G3	Tordenskjoldsgade	K4
Gammel Kongevej	B5	Nørre Søgade	G3	Tornebuskegade	H3
Gammel Strand	J4	Nørre Voldgade	H4	Torvegade	L5
Gammelmønt	J3	Nørrebrogade	C3	Valby Langgade	A6
Gammeltorv	H4	Nørregade	H3	Ved Stadsgraven	F6
Georg Brandes Plads	J2	Ny Adelgade	K4	Ved Stranden	K4
Godthåbsvej	B4	Ny Kongensgade	J5	Ved Vesterport	G5
Gothersgade	J3	Ny Østergade	K3	Vendersgade	G3
Gråbrødretorv	J4	Ny Vestergade	J5	Vermlandsgade	F6
Griffenfeldsgade	C3	Nybrogade	J5	Vester Farimagsgade	G4
Grønlandske Handels Plads	M4	Nygade	H4	Vester Søgade	C5
Grønningen	L1	Nyhavn	L4	Vester Voldgade	H5
Gyldenløvesgade	G4	Nytorv	H4	Vesterbrogade	G5
H C Ørsteds Vej	C4	Oslo Plads	K1	Vestergade	H5
Halmtorvet	C6	Østbanegade	K1	Vigerslev Allé	A6
Hammerichsgade	G5	Øster Allé	D2	Vimmelskaftet	J4
H C Andersens Boulevard	H5	Øster Farimagsgade	H2	Vindebrogade	J5
Hauser Plads	J3	Øster Søgade	H1	Vingårdsstræde	K4
Hausergade	J3	Øster Voldgade	J2	Vodroffsvej	C5
Havnegade	K5	Østerbrogade	E2	Vognmagergade	J3
Herluf Trolles Gade	L4	Østergade	K4	Wilders Plads	L5
Hestemøllestræde	H5	Otto Mönsteds Plads	J6		
Højbro Plads	J4	Overgaden Neden Vandet	L6		